AVOIDING
EMOTIONAL
DIVORCE

AVOIDING EMOTIONAL DIVORCE

John Lewis Lund Ed. D.

Hawkes Publishing, Inc.
P.O. Box 15711
Salt Lake City, Utah 84115

DEDICATION

To my wife, Bonnie Jeanne, a woman of extraordinary capacity for both work and love.

TABLE OF CONTENTS

CHAPTER 3

CHAPTER 4

CHAPTER 8

Learning the Love Language of the Task-Oriented Person _____ 83

CHAPTER 9

Learning the Love Language of the Touch-Oriented Person _____ 93

CHAPTER 10

PREFACE

The solution to the age-old human dilemma of loving and being loved in return involves knowledge, understanding, and a willingness to communicate in the love language of our mate. Often those involved in a relationship possess the willingness, but lack either the knowledge or understanding necessary to maintain emotional bonding.

I commend this volume to the reader with the sincere desire that it may be of great value in avoiding emotional divorce. While the suggestions are not a panacea, those who have chosen to follow such counsel are living examples of its practicality.

I also wanted this book to be a personal expression. It represents the experience accumulated over two decades of counseling and teaching. It is not my intent to appeal to the authority of others in order to establish the validity of its precepts—by design there are no footnotes. I refer instead to the pragmatic laboratory of life. The principles herein contained are justified only to the extent that they are useful. I have nevertheless attempted to give credit in the context of the work to those whose efforts required it, and I remain indebted to many scholars, past and present, for their observations and teachings. As the author, I assume full responsibility for the interpretations and views expressed.

CHAPTER ONE

ARE YOU EMOTIONALLY DIVORCED?

"I want a divorce!" These words spoken daily in kitchens, bedrooms, and family rooms, not only in America, but in much of the Western world may be screamed out in a moment of rage, or stated quietly on a note of desperation. However the message is conveyed, it forms a breech, whether it is mutually agreed upon by two intelligent people, or the decision of one mate who is past feeling any emotion for his spouse.

Emotional Divorce Defined

Webster defines divorce as "turning different ways," but physical and legal divorce are almost always preceded by emotional divorce, a period of estrangement which occurs long before lawyers are consulted. Emotional divorce is the state of turning away feelings or turning them off towards your mate. It is a condition where you may still care what happens "to" the person, but you cease caring "for" him because he is not meeting your expectations. One party or both feels unacceptable, unappreciated, and unwilling to give love.

1

With emotional divorce there comes a kind of resignation, a feeling that one mate is unwilling or unable to meet the needs of the other. Emotional closeness is gone, and the once available heart, no longer committed, has turned a different way. There is reluctance or refusal to rely on the spouse for love and affection. Often there is sex without love, or sometimes no sexual relationship at all.

Emotional divorce is the opposite of emotional oneness. The "common cause" that once united the couple has dissolved, leaving two people who share the same last name, the same house, the same children, the same bed, living in two separate emotional worlds.

Emotionally Divorced and Unaware

This book provides pragmatic information and practical insights in recognizing and responding to emotional needs. At the conclusion of a lecture titled, "Emotionally Divorced and Unaware," a lady came up to the lectern and requested a private moment.

In a nearby classroom she began to recount the events which had led to her feeling that she had been emotionally divorced from her husband for years. This woman was attractive, intelligent, and fluent in her verbal skills. She volunteered that she was in her late thirties and the mother of four children. Never once did she speak in a derogatory manner about her husband.

The tragedy was that her husband was totally unaware of her feelings. He must have been an incredibly insensitive human being not to pick up on her vibrations.

Paradoxically, this woman sincerely cared for her husband, but she felt emotionally divorced from him. Her insightful comments indicated a deeply considered analysis of their husband-wife relationship:

"I care for him as a person and as the father of our children," she said. "Without claiming perfection, I believe you would call me a devoted wife and mother. I sincerely attempt to meet his needs and be supportive. He is a wonderful man."

In some ways this relationship was classic. Because all of the husband's needs were met, he assumed she felt the same way he did.

"I've contemplated suicide,"she said, "but dismissed it because of what it would do to the children and to him."

Her pain was obvious.

"I have no one with whom I can discuss these things without jeopardizing my husband's position."

Controlled, yet tearfully, she spoke of her fidelity and loyalty to her husband. She shared her innermost confessions about her struggle to maintain mental purity. She rejected any intimation of a relationship which could lead to an affair with another man, although she had been aproached any number of times by men with this in mind. She was actively engaged in church and community programs and had served before the legislature as spokeswoman for a community cause. Few would perceive of this woman as anything other than fulfilled.

"On one occasion,"she related, "I actually packed by suitcase, put it in the car, made all the arrangements for my children, and left. I drove for two hours, only to return at 3:00 a.m. and quietly slip back into bed."

What kind of a man could be that unaware? I said to myself.

As if reading my mind, "My husband," she said, "is Dr. _____, Professor of Family Studies at _____."

I knew her husband by reputation. He was a colleague and a very popular lecturer. I had heard him speak myself and had met him on several occasions. I remembered a personal story he related about his wife and what it meant to be married to someone who was totally committed. I was stunned beyond belief. It was impossible to focus any longer on her story. I asked her if she would call me long distance and give me some time to react to her situation.

The thought flashed across my mind: Here I am in California lecturing on "Emotionally Divorced and Unaware," talking to a magnificent woman who is and has been emotionally divorced from her husband for years. This man is involved in the same profession as I yet he is oblivious to his wife's true feelings. Then lightning struck! Could my wife share these same feelings?

It is impossible to describe the terror of that moment. Could I be as ignorant of my wife's innermost thoughts about our relationship? Had she been sending messages that I had chosen to mistranslate in order to secure my own little world?

When I became aware of my surroundings, I found myself speeding to the airport. I dropped off the rent-a-car and made arrangements for an earlier flight home.

"Coach is all we have available in that flight, sir."

"That will be fine," I responded.

In my mind I thought that I would fly on the wing—on the outside of the plane—if it would get me home faster.

I telephoned my wife and prepared her for a discussion on my return. I was both nervous and abrupt.

"It sounds serious," she said.

"It is," I replied. "It's very serious. Do whatever you need to do with the children in order that we can talk. I mean really talk."

"Is it so serious," she asked in a low voice, "that you can't tell me over the phone?"

"Yes," I replied. "I must look into your eyes when we talk."

The jet plane seemed to lumber through the skies. I was without appetite. My mind was possessed by a single thought: Was my wife emotionally divorced from me?

At last the plane landed. To save an hour and a half, I drove the ninety miles from the intermediate airport rather than wait for a plane that would land eight miles from our home three hours later. I drove above the speed limit—not uncontrolled, but fearful of being stopped and detained in my quest for home.

Home! What awaited me there? I feared the worst. I thought of my lectures, my knowledge, my degrees, my experience, my published articles and books, and wondered what success could compensate if I had failed in my own home?

The car screeched to a halt in the driveway. I found my wife in the kitchen, and I was oblivious to all other things as I sat her down. With my hands cupping her face, I looked deep into her eyes, paused, and asked, "Are we emotionally divorced?"

"I hope not," she said. "Are you OK?"

I recounted to her the experience of the lady in California and noted the parallel in our lives. My wife was touched by my concern, and, frankly, quite relieved that it wasn't anything more serious. She commented that I had always had a flair for the dramatic, and she saw my overreaction as quite humorous.

My response, however, was one of incredible relief. I shall not forget that experience, nor the debt I owe a magnificent lady in California who taught me to internalize a sensitivity that I had been teaching others.

The lady from California called the following Tuesday. I asked for permission to involve a third party, a colleague who knew both her husband and me. I was sure the colleague would discretely be able to make her husband aware of her feelings without violating any confidences.

Apparently he was successful for later I met the learned professor in another city. He had changed positions and moved to another university in order to devote more time to what he preached. I saw him and his wife at a banquet a few years later. We never spoke, but she smiled at me and I knew that she had emotionally remarried her spouse.

What if it had been different for me? What if at that moment in the kitchen I had detected a fallen glance, a confession of not being in love or of infidelity? How does a person handle that kind of emotional bomb? The answer is, not very well. Frankly, it is a trauma equal to the death of a loved one.

The mate who is emotionally divorced arrives at that point after considerable frustration, and often, after having lived with a great deal of inner pain. Unmet expectations, the feelings of rejection or hostility take time to develop into a state of emotional divorce. And the marriage partner, though aware of problems, frequently misjudges their seriousness.

When the spouse who is still emotionally married first recognizes that his mate has emotionally divorced him, it takes time to accept it.

Take the following quizzes. Be honest in your responses, and be prepared to discuss your answers with your spouse.

Emotional Divorce Quiz

Has Your Mate Emotionally Divorced You?

1.   Are you called derogatory names by your mate each week?
2.   Are you frequently criticized (twice daily or more) about something?
3.   Do you feel used by your mate?
4.   Do you feel you are not acceptable to your mate as you now are?
5.   Do you find yourself trying to prove your love?
6.   Do you feel a lack of trust on the part of your mate?
7.   Do you feel appreciated in this relationship?
8.   Are you afraid to express your feelings for fear that the relationship will dissolve or that you will be ridiculed?
9.   Are you staying together for the sake of your children?
10. Do you feel emotionally divorced?

This quiz is not a precise tool, but it has proved to be a highly reliable indicator of concern.

[Count the number of "Yes" answers]   .

Score: 0- 3 = Normal concerns
          4- 6 = Definite problems
          7- 8 = Serious concerns
          9-10 = You have probably been emotionally divorced by
                 your mate

Have You Emotionally Divorced Your Mate?

1.   Are you frequently critical of your spouse (twice daily or more)?
2.   Do you swear and call you mate derogatory names (at least twice weekly)?
3.   Are you constantly frustrated about your relationship?
4.   Do you rely on others for the love and acceptance you would like to receive from your mate?
5.   Are you always forgetting the dates that are important to your mate?
6.   Are you unkind to your mate?
7.   Are you frequently sarcastic?
8.   Do you find yourself trying to punish your mate for past wrongs which he/she committed?
9.   Are you staying married for social reasons?
10. Do you have sexual intercourse with little or no emotion?

[Count the number of "Yes" answers]

Score: 0- 3 = Normal concerns
          4- 6 = Definite problems
          7- 8 = Serious concerns
          9-10 = You have probably emotionally divorced your mate

A Word About Willingness

Recognizing emotional divorce, either in one's self or in one's mate, is often the beginning of emotional remarriage. It is normal for a marriage or relationship to experience emotional divorce from time to time.

If the relationship is to survive the temporary state of emotional divorce and keep it from becoming a permanent divorce, both partners must be willing to work on the relationship. A relationship is the interaction of two parties. One person cannot make a relationship. When one party emotionally withdraws from a marriage and displays an unwillingness to pursue the relationship, there is precious little the emotionally abandoned mate can do.

It is amazing, however, what problems have been and can be overcome when both persons express a willingness to work on the problems. In fact, emotional remarriage is one of the great contemporary human adventures if both spouses are willing. Few lack capacity, but most lack awareness of how to stay emotionally married.

CHAPTER TWO

Awakening to Emotional Divorce

"I had no idea she felt our problems were that serious," is a common expression, and frequently it is only one of the marriage partners who feels emotionally divorced. Tragically, even after a legal divorce, it is not uncommon for one mate to remain emotionally married for years to the former spouse—some even die legally divorced, and yet emotionally married.

It is often easier to accept a death in the family than it is to reconcile oneself to emotional divorce. Ironically many health care professionals and family therapists have observed that the same steps which a terminally ill patient must go through in accepting their situation, also apply in accepting the reality of an emotionally dead relationship. One divorcee stated it this way: "It would have been easier to accept his death, because I could have worked through it and gone on with my life. Seeing him every time he picks up the kids is a constant reminder, and makes it more difficult to adjust."

The stages of accepting death, divorce, and similar serious trauma involve shock, denial, anger, depression, bargaining, acceptance, and resignation. Most people, with some support, are able to work through all of these steps and make whatever adjustments are necessary. A few never do, however, and they use the trauma as an excuse for avoiding responsibility for not taking control of the rest of their life.

A State of Shock and Denial

It is one thing to have a relationship where both partners are aware that they are emotionally divorced, and quite another when only one marriage partner is emotionally divorced and aware of it.

The spouse who is oblivious to the emotional divorce is sometimes dramatically shocked when he discovers the alienation of his mate. Whether the news of the emotional divorce comes by a phone call from a friend, a letter, a tearful confession, logic, or "catching them in the act," the reaction is one of shock.

When patients are first told they have terminal cancer or some other terminal illness, they are stunned. They just can't believe it is that serious. Obviously a mistake has been made. There has been a confusion in the files or the tests have been incorrectly administered or interpreted. Because many refuse to accept the findings of one physician, they go from doctor to doctor, from pillar to post, from faith healer to food fanatic, refusing to accept reality.

Eventually they will simply avoid anyone or anything that reminds them of the disease. By choosing not to accept it, and not to talk about it, they hope to erase its existence. They live in a fantasy world and surround themselves with things or with other people who will humor them. After all, they reason, the doctors don't know everything. "Maybe I'm an exception. This just can't be happening to me. Someone has made a mistake. Tell me it is someone else."

Very often the same disbelief and shock accompany the awareness of both physical and emotional divorce.

A State of Anger

In the case of terminal illness, as with emotional divorce, after the initial shock is over, there is often a period of anger. Why did he die? Why did he leave me? Why was he unfaithful?

This hostility is normal but it can be dangerous. During the past years in the United States, a significant number of murders committed involved husbands or wives killing each other. When ex-husbands and ex-wives and estranged spouses are included, the number of murders almost doubles. Suicides among terminally ill patients or those with terminally ill relationships are also significant. This is serious business.

Usually anger is first directed at others: "Why would God allow this to happen to me?" Many people become angry with God, questioning their faith and challenging the justice of Diety.

If there has been infidelity, then the "other man" or "other woman" becomes the focus of frustration: "If he would move away or just leave my mate alone, all would be well." However, the other person is not the problem, only a symptom of emotional divorce, a target for hostility.

Soon the accusing finger comes to rest on the unfaithful mate: "It's all your fault. You did this to me. I will never forgive you. I'll make you pay for this. I want a divorce."

But frequently the anger is directed inward: "It's all my fault. I'm a failure. What did I do wrong?" Self-doubt and fear are poised, ready to rob us of confidence in any relationship.

A State of Depression

It is during this stage of prolonged depression that suicides sometimes occur, both in the terminally ill and the emotionally divorced. Few people resort to such extreme measures, but many permit such thoughts to cross their minds.

There appears to be a certain amount of grief that these persons work through, depending on the extent of their emotional involvement. Some never leave this state of depression and take it with them to the grave, never able to fully recover from the heartache, frustration, and disappointment of it all. They often become cynical and bitter about life, and question their value and self-worth.

On the brighter side, the majority of people work through their depression or learn to cope with it, and begin looking for solutions.

A State of Bargaining

For the terminally ill patient, there is often an effort made to bargain with God for their life. With the emotionally divorced, the point of seeing a marriage counselor is to try to make it right, to embrace a philosophy of "Where do we go from here?" For the emotionally divorced, this can be a very productive state if the causes for the emotional divorce can be analyzed, understood, and dealt with. Third party professionals can be of enormous value at this point in helping the emotionally divorced sort through their basic concerns, which almost always have to do with communication, money, sex, religion, children, in-laws, recreation, and friends. Underlying these focal points are the more basic questions of love, belonging, acceptance, appreciation, and personal security.

A State of Acceptance

Once a person has passed the initial shock and worked through the denial, anger, and depression involved with emotional divorce, he is prepared to look at the realistic alternatives:

1.   Physical divorce

2.   Staying together for reasons other than emotional fulfillment
3.   Creating or sustaining a destructive marital environment
4.   Emotional remarriage

Physical Divorce

Before physical divorce is decided upon by one or both parties, these things ought to be considered:

1.   It requires nearly the same amount of emotional energy to make a second marriage work as it does the first one or the third one.
2.   No one is perfect. Everyone has problems, strengths, weaknesses, and concerns. The real question is one of coping. Are your mate's characteristics within your coping range? They *have* been; could they be again?
3.   With professional help, could adjustments be made in the relationship so as to satisfy both husband and wife?
4.   Is it more productive to attempt to solve the problem or to abandon the relationship?
5.   Are the adjustments you would have to make the same as for any relationship?
6.   Is infatuation or love with an extra-marital partner clouding your ability to examine the true merits of your current marriage?

Relationships are really two-party agreements, and the marriage contract is just that, a contract. Each party agrees to certain terms and conditions. But if one party is unwilling, there is little or nothing the other party can do. Some people are indeed much happier when they divorce.

Hundreds, however, wish they had never left their first marriage. Their second or third marriage was not the answer either.

Staying Together for Reasons Other Than Emotional Fulfillment

Staying together for reasons other than emotional fulfillment is an alternative to divorce having many merits, and there are a great number of couples who have chosen it. These couples accept emotional divorce and look upon marriage as an arrangement, in some cases as a business affair. They agree to be kind to one another, to avoid hostility, and to cooperate. The motivation may be religious, professional, political, social, or even psychological, but they agree to maintain the relationship and allow considerable freedom for each partner. They live in two worlds. They may share the same children, the same house, and even sleep together, but they remain emotionally divorced. Nevertheless, their relationship is adequate.

Creating or Sustaining a Destructive Marriage

Unmet expectations always generate frustration. In turn, frustration takes many forms—criticism, backbiting, namecalling, physical abuse, alcoholism, infidelity, and on and on. Often, frustration turned inward creates numerous psychosomatic disorders including hypochondria, ulcers, etc.

Children raised in this kind of hostile environment invariably suffer the natural emotional consequences it generates, including various neuroses, insecurities, and unhealthy self-images. In situations such as this, divorce doesn't solve the problem, it only separates the parents.

Counseling is recommended to help the individuals work through their frustration and come to an understanding of why they behave the way they do. A marriage that is in a constant state of war is not a marriage, but an experience in masochism. There are things worse than divorce. One of them is marriage which destroys both the children and parents and fills them with hate, hostility, and a bitter attitude toward life.

The real tragedy is that trained family therapists are available to help people who have real problems but often they are not consulted. The excuse that "those who need it the most usually can't afford it" is more a commentary on a person's value system than an accurate appraisal of reality. When someone's life is in danger, money is seldom a consideration. The physician with a specialty is called immediately. When a marriage relationship is about to die, financial consideration often seems more important than the health of the relationship. Frequently, however, counseling costs less than divorce.

Should not both the health of the body and the emotional health of the individual be considered above financial concerns? More and more, health care plans carry provisions whereby a significant portion of the qualified counselor's fees are paid. The business sector recognizes that an employee from a stable emotional environment is an important investment.

There are answers, there are solutions, there are programs, but willingness to seek and accept counsel is necessary if change is to take place.

Emotional Remarriage

One of the most exciting adventures in life is emotional remarriage. Probably no greater satisfaction can come to a family therapist than to be instrumental in seeing a relationship come together because it is built on solid principles of emotional health.

All therapists recognize that the initial emotional bonding involving courting probably took place before the wedding ceremony. One wise observer has noted that too often the wedding alter marks the end of dating instead of the beginning of a life-long courtship. Unfortunately, we soon forget those patterns and become immersed in schedules pertaining to the "bread and butter" existence of everyday pressures.

Premarital courting was a time of sharing, caring, planning, and dreaming, a time of putting you best foot forward, of being kind and thoughtful. Whatever principles were brought into focus to obtain emotional bonding before marriage are the same principles needed to maintain emotional bonding after marriage. In other words, even though the circumstances change after marriage, the principles of kindness and consideration do not change if emotional bonding is to be maintained or re-established.

If there is one thing I have come to appreciate as a marriage and family therapist it is the fact that human beings are capable of changing their behavior. Knowledge, information, and understanding often bring a change of perspective and a subsequent change of expectations for their mate. Emotional remarriage is possible. I have witnessed marriage after marriage experience this change and re-establish emotional bonding. You can do it.

Summary

Accepting emotional divorce is never easy. It is normal for one to pass through the stages of shock, denial, anger, depression, bargaining, and acceptance. Once a person accepts emotional divorce, he or she has basically four alternatives: 1) physical divorce, 2) staying together for reasons other than emotional fulfillment, 3) creating or sustaining a destructive marital environment, or 4) emotional remarriage. The latter is by far the most satisfying, and perhaps the most challenging solution. Nevertheless, emotional remarriage has been accomplished by thousands of couples who stand ready to testify to the rewards of such efforts.

CHAPTER THREE

Removing the Barriers to Emotional Remarriage

For a couple or an individual who has grown out of love, emotional remarriage requires trust, selflessness, commitment, time, and effective communication. The need to curtail criticism will be dealt with in a subsequent chapter.

Checklist: Preparation for Emotional Remarriage

		Husband		Wife	
		Yes	No	Yes	No
1.	Am I willing to sincerely commit myself to a genuine effort to emotionally remarry?	☐	☐	☐	☐
2.	Am I willing to spend the time necessary to re-establish emotional bonding?	☐	☐	☐	☐
3.	Am I willing to abstain from criticizing my mate?	☐	☐	☐	☐
4.	Am I willing to communicate my true feelings and expectations to my mate?	☐	☐	☐	☐

5.   Am I willing to seek professional   ☐ ☐   ☐ ☐
     counseling for the sake of emotional
     remarriage?

6.   Am I willing to forgive my mate for   ☐ ☐   ☐ ☐
     past wrongs committed against our
     relationship?

7.   Am I willing to set aside any con-   ☐ ☐   ☐ ☐
     flicting relationship in order to focus
     on the marriage?

Only after a plane has been properly serviced, supplied with fuel, etc., is it ready for take-off. So it is with emotional remarriage. If there is a lack of willingness in any of these areas, success of the flight is jeopardized, and if there is a lack of willingness in two or more of these areas, the marriage will have to remain on the ground until attitudes and events clear the way for take-off.

The Trust Level

If emotional remarriage is to occur, trust must be re-established in the relationship. It is true that trust must be earned by responsible behavior, but it is also true that sufficient freedom and latitude must be granted in order to foster trust.

When someone has been "burned" in a marriage relationship, proper conduct is a must if the trust level is to be reinstated. Some have felt that it was not necessary to alter their life style in order to rebuild their mate's trust. This is a fallacy. The initial stages of emotional remarriage are very delicate. The marriage is on trial. It is a time of probation, a time of testing the relationship to see whether the cautious heart can be fully recommitted.

Emotional issues are quite predictable when you understand the frame of reference even though there are those who want to believe that the emotions are totally unpredictable and illogical. Because someone does not understand the logic does not mean that the emotion is illogical. From the standpoint of emotional security emotions are very logical. Because trust makes emotional sense, it is foolish to argue that behavior does not have to be altered if trust is to be re-established.

Assume that a husband has had an affair with a secretary at the office. But when he and the secretary analyze their situation, they determine they have too much to lose in their individual marriages, and so they break off the affair.

The husband of the secretary remained unaware of the affair. The boss's wife suspected something was wrong because of her husband's behavior, but was never able to prove it until one night she accused her husband and he confessed to infidelity.

After shedding tears and pouring out their grief, the couple decided to go forward with their marriage. The husband had been in the habit of taking his coffee break with the secretary with whom he had had the affair. After all, they had been friends before the affair, there would be little chance of affair's recurrence, so why shouldn't they continue to be friends? Why should the wife be so unreasonable as to insist that they not share coffee breaks any more and that they not dance together at the office party? Perhaps the wife even insists that the secretary be fired. The matter could be even more complicated if the husband picks up the secretary in a car pool and is often alone in the car with her.

When his wife objects, even though the husband has assured her that a recurrence is virtually impossible, he may wonder why his wife doesn't trust him. Leaving the car pool does not make economic sense, but it makes a great deal of emotional sense. The husband must avoid any situation which raises the issue of his integrity. He should leave the car pool and make every effort to be above reproach in his conduct with the secretary. If he is unwilling to alter his life style, he is seriously endangering the possibility that sufficient trust can be established for emotional remarriage.

A man who was involved in a similar situation found himself alone at the office with the woman in question. She had no other way to go home and she asked if he would please give her a ride home since they lived just two blocks from each other.

"Why don't you take my car and go home," he suggested, "I have some things I need to do here at the office and I can find another way home later."

The secretary took the car home and the man later called a cab. Economic sense? No, but it made considerable emotional sense.

Imagine the wife's emotional response if he had taken his secretary home. Doubt, fear, hurt feelings, and lack of trust may have initiated an argument. Would there have been tears? Would the entire issue of trust have been raised again?

Listen to the arguments of the husband:

"Am I going to be on trial for the rest of my life? I've told you the affair is over, why don't you believe me? I resent the fact that you can't get over the mistake I made and deal with it intelligently. I'm an adult, yet I feel like I'm being treated like a child. I've told you that you don't have anything to worry about. You've got to learn to trust me. If you can't trust me, then maybe we ought to get a divorce."

The wife responds:

"How do I know you won't do it again? How can I trust you when you keep meeting her? You always have a good excuse for being together."

By letting the secretary use his car—alone—this entire argument was avoided and trust was increased when the husband related the circumstance to his wife.

This is a clear demonstration of an effort made to reinstate the level of trust necessary for emotional remarriage. His consideration for his wife's feelings increases her confidence in him and pays emotional dividends far in excess of the cab fare home.

This kind of effort, consideration, and thoughtfulness is necessary to raise the level of trust.

Trustworthiness

There is also a question of being able to trust someone with your feelings. If I tell you how I really feel, will you make fun of me? Will you ridicule me? Not only can I trust you sexually, but can I trust you emotionally? Are you capable of handling my trust, or will you play games of emotional duplicity, requiring one standard of trust from me and another for yourself?

Take the following quiz to see if you are emotionally trustworthy.

Trust Level Quiz

		Yes	No
.1	During the last year, have you made your spouse the brunt of any jokes?	☐	☐
2.	Have you discussed your marital sex life with anyone other than a professional counselor?	☐	☐
3.	Have you revealed your spouse's weaknesses to friends or family?	☐	☐
4.	Have you told secrets dealing with your marriage that you promised not to tell?	☐	☐
5.	Have you told stories that put your spouse in a negative or embarrassing light?	☐	☐
6.	When you enter into an argument or a serious discussion, do you bring up past relationships or love affairs?	☐	☐
7.	Are you flirtatious?	☐	☐
8.	Has your conduct with the opposite sex been called into question by your spouse, family, or friends?	☐	☐
9.	Are there reasons why you should not be trusted?	☐	☐
10.	Are you a dishonest person?	☐	☐

On the basis of the number of yes answers, the following guide gives an indication of your trustworthiness.

0- 3 Yes answers = normal concerns
4- 6 Yes answers = needs definite improvement
7-10 Yes answers = you are not an emotionally trustworthy person and you need to see a professional counselor

Selflessness

It is unfortunate that most wedding ceremonies include the phrase, "Do you take this man and do you take this woman?" Many couples then spend the rest of their lives "taking" each other. How much more indicative of the true marriage relationship are these words: "Do you give yourself to this man and do you give yourself to this woman?" If these words were a part of the ceremony the element of selflessness would be introduced at the onset of the marriage.

A number of marriages end in emotional divorce because of selfishness. Often one member of the marriage has to have everything his or her way. Such individuals are the ones who always have to be right. They have to have things their way or they won't play.

"You Give, I Take"

This kind of marriage is called "You give and I take." As long as the health, desire, and stamina of the one "giving" holds out, the marriage purrs right along. At some point, however, the one who is giving will begin to run short of emotional resources. He will also run out of physical stamina and the marriage will be in trouble. Actually, the marriage was in trouble from the first day, for like the explosion of a time bomb, it was only a question of time.

Nevertheless, responsibility for such a marriage rests on the shoulders of both parties. Somewhere, each assented to or acquiesced in their role, and by the time the "taking" partner realized that the "giving" partner had emotionally and often physically "burned out," the resentment felt by the "giving" partner was so great that the marriage was irretrievably broken.

The natural consequence of the "you give and I take" marriage is eventually that the "giving" spouse begins to resent the "taking" partner and the resentment takes the form of emotional hostility, anger, ulcers, or total emotional deadness.

The problem of the "taking" partner is that he or she was not "far-sighted" enough to look to the long-term effect of his own selfishness. Such individuals suffer from a myopic selfishness which disables them as contributing marriage partners.

Appropriate Selfishness

The "giving" partner's problem is that he or she is not appropriately selfish. There is such a thing as appropriate selfishness, and it has to do with a person taking proper personal care of his physical, emotional, and intellectual needs. You can be no better as a marriage partner than you are as an individual. After all, one is first and foremost an individual, a self, an independent identity, a unique person. Although an individual will have many relationships during the course of his or her existence, none will be longer or more intense than the relationship with self.

What does it mean to be appropriately selfish? It means that one maintains a program of proper diet, sleep, and exercise sufficient to cope with the stresses of life.

It is unrealistic to assume that you will always be able to rise above the coping line. There is a certain amount of frustration, upset, and physical fatigue that is part of living. However, when these become the rule and not the exception, the time for self-examination and change has arrived. Someone is not appropriately selfish.

"I don't have time to take a class at the university or to be involved in community activities," some will say. No, you have the time; what you don't have is a priority system that allows for appropriate selfishness.

Total selfishness is a tragedy that can only be contrasted with the tragedy of the total loss of identity which often results from not being appropriately selfish. Giving of self is a need—it can even be a virtue. However, when it becomes an excuse for sloppy personal appearance and low self-esteem, it has become a vice.

The Ability to Receive

Of what value is a gift if a person chooses not to receive the gift? The answer: "It is of little value." An important part of any relationship is the ability of each partner to receive what the other has to give. A synonym for "receive" is "accept." Acceptance is the most basic human emotional need. After the basic physical needs of air, food, water, clothing, shelter, and physical security, comes the emotional need for acceptance.

When you care for someone deeply and sincerely, there springs forth a desire to give of yourself. Sometimes that desire is so strong and compelling that it manifests itself in a shower of affection. Poems are written, flowers are purchased, songs are composed to express the feelings of love. What frustration then exists when the loved one has eyes, but chooses not to see; has ears, but chooses not to hear? The object of the love does not receive the gifts of self offered by the loving one.

The art of receiving is the art of being gracious. The ability to receive is the ability to be appreciative.

Some have mistakenly thought they must return like for like. This is seldom the case. Most great artists or poets do not demand equal performance, just equal commitment. One such talented person explained to his wife: "If I write a deeply moving poem that expresses the song of my soul, I do not expect you to reciprocate. I only ask that you read it or listen to me intently as I read it. It is my offering of love."

The wife in this situation felt a little depressed and obligated by his gift to do some great thing in return. Her reactions, therefore, to his "gifts of love" were consistently depressing. He felt more and more frustrated, and she felt pressure to do something, but she did not know how or what. By the time they came for counseling he had emotionally divorced her. He had stopped writing poems for her and had stopped sending her love signals. She was absolutely bewildered.

Twice in three weeks I instructed her in the art of being a good receiver. Fortunately she learned her lessons well. The following is a recapitulation of our sessions.

The Art of Receiving

"In football, you cannot have any great passers unless you have some great receivers. It is the same in marriage. Receiving involves intensity of interest. A player who takes his eyes off of the ball invariably drops it. When a love message is sent, a wise receiver concentrates on the message.

"If you are involved in seven different things at once, set them aside and give 100% attention for a few minutes. Half-hearted attention is an insult, a form of rejection, and will most likely be interpreted by the passer as disinterest or tolerance. Tolerance is not acceptance, appreciation, or love.

"There will always be reasons why you can't give 100% attention; i.e., children, schedule, others who demand time. But with each reason, a message of rejection is sent. Reasons become excuses. You might as well say, 'I don't have time for you. Why don't you go and find someone else who is interested and who has the time?'

"Is that what you wanted to say?"

"Oh, no," she said, "but sometimes I am genuinely under pressure. I think he needs to understand that, and not expect me to drop everything for him. I feel I am being tested all the time. Every time I am busy, I think he is putting me on trial. Will I choose him, or the other activities? If I ever choose anything but him, then I have failed the test and he goes off sulking."

"I am sure that happens, but there is a way you can receive the message and at the same time honestly express the pressure you feel. Give me a typical situation and I will attempt a response."

"The other night one of the children forgot until 5:45 p.m. that he was assigned refreshments for the cub scout meeting. The local store closes at 6:00 p.m. and our cub scout had to be at the meeting by 6:30 p.m. My husband walked in and says, 'Honey, may I share something with you?' There I was on trial. Do I choose him or our child?"

"What did you do?"

"I told him I would when I got back. I could tell he was disappointed, but he should have gone to the store and taken our cub scout to the meeting."

"Did you tell him that?"

"No, I was showing him that I loved him and our family by not bothering him with it."

"Let me respond with a suggestion and a recommendation for the situation you just described. Remember to concentrate on the message and give the message 100% attention."

"But how?" she inquired.

"I'm coming to that. When your husband said, 'Honey, may I share something with you?' You should have gone over to him, put your arms around him, and said, 'Yes, my love, you may share everything with me,' and then you should have given him a great big kiss. Before he had a chance to recover, you could have explained the problem, invited his help, and set up a definite time to 'share something,' even if it had to be at 12:00 midnight. If you had acted this way, he would have been satisfied and you may have just enlisted his support for your situation. There are two very important points in this illustration. First, you received his message by acknowledging, with your body, his presence. In other words, you focused on the messenger. Secondly, you gave him 100% attention for 30 seconds and you acknowledged the importance of his message by setting up a midnight rendezvous. Now, I want you to go home and practice these two things: 1) focusing on the message, and 2) giving 100% attention to the messenger. I'll see you next week. Good luck."

After a week, she returned to my office.

"Well, how was it? How did you do on your assignment?" I asked.

"I really did quite well. I was amazed, as a matter of fact, that I did as well as I did."

"Tell me about it."

"The first thing I must tell you is that he was very suspicious of my behavior. I'm sure he was taken back. He seemed cautious and a little withdrawn. I got the feeling that he thought that I was being phony with him, but he went along anyway. I was really intense; when I felt a message was coming, I looked him right in the eyes. He was threatened by my intensity and I could see he thought I was overdoing it, but he didn't complain."

"Were there any emergencies this last week?"

"No, not really."

"Great! Are you ready for lesson number two on the art of receiving?"

"I think so."

"Fine. I want you to ask him to write you a poem."

"Do I dare?"

"Yes, you dare because we are going to talk about expressing appreciation as a part of the art of receiving. When you receive the poem, it may be that he will just leave it on the dresser for you. Read it, commit one or two lines to memory, or even a phrase that strikes your fancy, call him on the phone, and ask him if he would read it to you that night—because you want to remember it as it came from his lips. He may be suspicious, but do it anyway. Later, when the two of you are alone, focus on the message and give 100% attention to the messenger. He ought to be used to that by then. After he has read it to you, tell him what your favorite part is, and quote the line or phrase you have memorized. Reach out and take his hand and look deeply into his eyes and say, 'Thank you. I sincerely appreciate that poem. And what's more, I have a request to make. Would it be possible, for my birthday or maybe for Valentine's Day, for you to compile all the poems you have ever written and have them bound into a single volume for me?' How do you think he will respond?"

"I imagine that he would be overwhelmed. He'd probably question my sincerity."

"You have brought up the final point in the art of receiving which is sincerity. You must be yourself, and you must be able to back up what you say with genuine concern or you will endanger your relationship. Sincerity is the glue that sticks what you say to the heart and mind. That's why it is important for you to translate everything we have talked about into your style. I have given you not just a solution to a particular problem, but a pattern in dealing with your mate's love language:

1.   Focus on the message
2.   Give 100% attention to the messenger
3.   Express appreciation
4.   Be sincere

For the next two months, why don't you take a line from one of his poems and, once a week, send it to work with him in a note in one of his pockets. Be creative. Think of ways of expressing appreciation."

I saw the couple three months later and they were emotionally remarried because she had learned the art of receiving.

CHAPTER FOUR

Criticism and Emotional Remarriage

A major obstacle to emotional remarriage is the tendency to be critical of one's mate and of oneself. These critical tendencies did not begin with marriage, they developed with the personality and are almost always a reflection of or reaction to one's experience of growing up.

We live in a highly critical society, and in addition to the home as a primary influence in a critical disposition, society reinforces all tendencies to be critical. In fact, criticism is held up as a virtue in many professions; i.e., the art critic, the music critic, the literary critic, the wine connoisseur, the gourmet, the sports broadcaster, the news analyst, the stockbroker, etc.

What could be more natural than to have a critical disposition? Isn't the world of science founded on this very principle? Doesn't the scientific method require criticism? Indeed, doesn't the very advancement of the frontiers of knowledge require an almost religious devotion to criticism as the means of improvement?

Criticism: Enemy to Emotional Bonding

Criticism may be incredibly effective and necessary to both the advancement of knowledge and the scientific method, but it is an enemy to emotional bonding. Yet criticism is so much a part of our life style that it is difficult to imagine a relationship without it.

It is a swordlike weapon. It can be used to harvest grain, to chop wood, and for a thousand other useful purposes. However, like the sword, most often criticism is used in war. It maims, injures, and destroys emotional bonding, even in the closest of family relationships.

Criticism Defined

Criticism is the verbal or non-verbal finding of fault. It implies disapproval. Often it involves fixing blame or responsibility for an error. The net result is loss of self-worth, a weakened self-concept, and a feeling of being unappreciated, unacceptable, or "put down."

As it pertains to relationships criticism has many names. Nagging and fault finding are two of the most common. Sarcasm and the pun represent humorous and more sophisticated forms of criticism. Nevertheless, the effect on the one who is the object of the sarcasm is the same—self-concept is diminished.

"I like your hair, dear. I wonder how it would look if you combed it?"

It's a funny line. Everyone laughs. Even the one who is the brunt of the joke may laugh, but inside they bleed a little and feel less worthy as a human being.

Analysis, appraisal, and evaluation often mask more subtle forms of criticism which are no less devastating to the one being judged.

Things can be evaluated and ideas can be subjected to the scientific method, but people are human beings with basic emotional needs of acceptance, love, belonging, and appreciation. The most self-actualized person on earth subjected to a consistent diet of criticism will eventually retreat to a fantasy world, become a hermit, or fall apart emotionally.

Criticism: Thief of Acceptance

The most basic human emotional need is acceptance, both self-acceptance and acceptance from others. Whether the need is called "love" or "belonging," it is translated as acceptance.

What is so devastating about criticism is that it robs a person of acceptance. Criticism is rejection. You cannot continue to bombard a human being with rejection without destroying his perceived self-worth as well as his perceived value to others.

Experience as a family court commissioner and as a marriage and family counselor leads me to the conclusion that criticism has robbed more relationships of love than any other single factor, because it attacks the very foundation of acceptance upon which the emotional bonding in a relationship is based.

Think of a relationship free from pernicious criticism. How would it be? Think of a relationship where criticism in any form was used so sparingly that weeks and months would pass without a "put down," a cutting remark, or even a "constructively critical" comment.

You may find yourself becoming immediately defensive, rationalizing your particular use of criticism. But in actuality there is no personal criticism which is justified.

No "Constructive" Criticism

Some people like to talk about *constructive criticism.* Unfortunately criticism is always *de*structive, although there may be times when it is necessary to destroy or to tear down an improperly built structure. On such occasions, it should be called *destructive* criticism. The two words "constructive" and "criticism" contradict each other. Yet, if we hear the two words together long enough, we come to believe that we really understand them. We cannot build and tear down at the same time. To construct is to build, to edify, and to uplift. To criticize is to blame, to find fault, to disapprove, and to censure. If there is ever to be any construction, it can only follow the destruction created by the criticism.

Yes, there are times when being critical is truly in someone's best interest. But where is the husband, wife, or child about whom it can be honestly said that they need to be criticized daily? A single aspirin can be helpful; an entire bottle can kill you. A little vaccine can prevent an illness; too much vaccine will destroy the very thing it is intended to save.

Criticism is a Cancer

Has the cancer of criticism consumed so much of your language that you are past the point of a cure? Has the disease robbed you of the power to resist? Criticism gnaws at the sinews of a marriage until it leaves the relationship lifeless. It creates deep wounds and makes enemies of husbands and wives.

So many people have lived with intense criticism for so long that they cannot imagine not being criticized. They were seriously criticized as a child; why should marriage be any different? They have been criticized until they believe they are worthless, and because they are infected with the disease, they pass it on to their children. Where then is the end of it?

Most of us greatly resent any criticism that comes to our spouse or children, and we are quick to jump to their defense. Why then do we turn on them ourselves? Why do we persist in being critical? The answer is that we act out of habit, frustration, and anger, and sometimes we are deluded, thinking that we are acting in their best interest, to help them change their behavior.

Criticism Doesn't Change Behavior

The irony of ironies is that many people criticize in order to change behavior, yet criticism only antagonizes, alienates, and, at best, only temporarily controls behavior. Criticism does not change behavior.

Verbal criticism is actually a description of the critic's rejection of the person. Non-verbal criticism, such as a frown, also communicates non-acceptance. And change does not occur by means of a negative verbal description nor does a frown inspire change.

Whether the rejection is communicated verbally or non-verbally, the person being criticized will most often reject the one who is doing the criticizing instead of rejecting the unaccepted behavior.

Change occurs when the motivation comes from within. Criticism is an outside force that may achieve a degree of control, but control is not change. A sponge, for example, can be made to conform to whatever outside pressure is exerted upon it. Yet as soon as the pressure is released, the sponge will assume its previous shape. So it is with the pressure of criticism. You may be able to temporarily impose conformity, but as soon as you leave, the person will revert to previous behavior. Your criticism is actually counter-productive because it weakens a person's self concept as well as his self-confidence, and lessens the probability for real change.

Threat, fear, and criticism have been used for centuries to control human behavior, but meanwhile, they create an adverse relationship. One observer has noted that grandparents get along better with their grandchildren than with their own children, because they seem to be more loving and far less critical with their grandchildren. This has led to a humorous saying: "Grandparents and grandchildren are natural allies because they share a common enemy."

Could any mother, looking upon her day-old child, desire to create an adverse relationship with that child? Yet mothers often make remarks like: "You are always leaving your coat on the floor. Why don't you pick it up? Do you want to live in a pig pen?"

This is negative behavior, and the speaker has made the

individual *aware* of her disapproval and his weakness. In effect she told him that he is a sloppy person.

"Why don't you ever think before you turn on the TV? Don't you know it will wake up the baby?"

Now the speaker makes him feel dumb.

"I wish, just for once, you would do your jobs without being yelled at."

Now he thinks he's lazy.

With each criticism, the self-concept is perceived and he thinks of himself as a sloppy, dumb, lazy teenager. Like Dr. Frankenstein, we assist in creating the very image we want to destroy.

Love and acceptance change behavior. Criticism does not.

Coaches who exert the most profound positive effect upon their athletes are the ones who genuinely love the players, accept them, and inspire them to greatness.

Those coaches who use fear, intimidation, ridicule, criticism, sarcasm, and other belittling ploys seldom inspire anything but resentment, hostility, and poor self-image.

Is the marriage relationship any different?

Why Do People Criticize?

People usually criticize because someone is not measuring up to expectations, and the critic is frustrated. The truth of the matter is that much criticism is based on frustration—we want our loved ones to do what we want them to do. Therefore we lash out, nag, gripe, complain, cry, swear, and attack them.

Ironically, while our lips drip with venom, our hearts are hoping that someone will love us, care for us, respect us, accept us, appreciate us, and want to be with us, and yes, even overlook our weaknesses.

There are more productive ways of communicating frustration, and they work. Criticism doesn't remove frustration. It's a bandaid, not a cure. If the critical person does not find positive ways of communicating frustration, he will invariably increase his critical nature and drive all his loved ones away, and thus increase his frustration until he explodes into tears of resentment or sulks in silent oblivion where hostility dwells.

For every example of the positive effects of criticism, there are one hundred broken marriages, broken homes, and broken lives. Criticism is a cancer. Its psychological spin-offs are myriad in their devastations.

Those Who Criticize to Belittle

There are people who do not criticize to change behavior or to vent frustration. They criticize to belittle others. In their sick minds, they gather comfort by putting others down. They are sociopathic in their criticism, and their egos feed on the faults of others. They are obsessed with bad-mouthing everyone and everything, hoping to avoid the responsibility of making any painful change in their own lives.

Those Who Criticize the Most are the Most Sensitive to Criticism

Many observations over the years have confirmed the suspicion that those who are the most critical are also the most sensitive to criticism. Their criticism of others is often a ploy to divert attention from themselves—from the weaknesses they fear others will notice.

Such individuals often explode into anger, and yell and scream far beyond what criticism of the behavior might seem to justify. They want to reserve to themselves the right of being critical of others. Occasionally, you will see a "boss" of this type who surrounds himself with "yes men," and spews out criticism. Yet he lives in a fantasy world, for he has neither the love, nor the respect and productivity he might otherwise enjoy.

Some families are this same way.

Refuge from the Storm

It is doubtful that criticism can be erased from the mentality of our society—a mentality dominated in many ways by the scientific method. You may not be successful in changing your outside environment to a less critical one, though it might be fun to try, but there is something you can do about your critical nature as far as your marriage is concerned.

Why not allow your home to be a refuge from such storms? Think of your mate as a haven, a peaceful retreat, the ever-quiet eye of the hurricane.

What would a husband-wife relationship be without criticism? Try promising your wife you will never say a critical word about her, make her the brunt of jokes, nor in any way speak unkindly of her, or betray your relationship, and ask her to promise the same in return.

What confidence it gives a woman to know that when other men are making fun of their wives or complaining about their weaknesses, their cooking, homemaking, lovemaking, short-comings, and faults, her name is safe.

When women get together and begin to belittle their husbands, what security there is in knowing that your name will not be mentioned!

Oh, it isn't because you have no faults; faults are self-evident. It isn't because she wouldn't be justified. She simply does not speak ill of you—nor do you speak ill of her—because of your loyalty to one another.

If you have recently married, make this pledge of loyalty one to another. If you are emotionally divorced, but are sincerely willing to attempt an emotional remarriage, take this pledge and live by it:

> I promise, as your mate, that I will never speak ill of you to friend, family, or stranger. I will not embarrass or belittle you in front of others, nor will I be critical of you in your absence. I

will not discuss our personal problems with anyone without your permission. This is my pledge to you.

How Do You Overcome Being a Critical Person?

A person has taken the first step in overcoming criticism when he feels a sincere desire to overcome it. Much like dieting, overcoming the compulsion is a significant portion of the struggle, and discouragement is an ever-present risk.

Start by stopping. For a period of twenty-four hours, refrain from criticizing yourself and anything else.

It isn't as easy as it sounds. You may be your own worst enemy. Self-criticism is a self-defeating behavior.

People often criticize themselves in the hope that others will come to their emotional rescue. Most of the time when we criticize ourselves, we are really seeking acceptance.

Imagine that someone comes to you and says, "Did you make that dress?"

"It's just a rag," you reply. "I threw it together."

To protect yourself you tear yourself down before someone else has a chance. How would you feel if they agreed?

The kind of a comment we really seek is, "Oh no! That's not a rag, it's really nice. I wish I could sew like that."

The majority of people do not succeed in their first attempt to go without criticizing for twenty-four hours. Do not be discouraged if in the next few minutes or hours, you find yourself being critical. But the moment you slip, start your twenty-four hours over again. You must not criticize your spouse, your children, parents, co-workers, the boss, or anyone—including the government. And if you will be doing any driving in the next twenty-four hours, it may be particularly difficult. Phone calls are also dangerous. And watch out when you are hungry or under any sort of time pressure. Getting the kids in bed may just push you over the line!

There are a few people whose employment outside the home requires them to be critical; for example building inspectors, supervisors, etc. These special cases are exempt as long as they are on the job, and as long as the criticism relates directly to the work. Everyone else will be under the challenge to go for twenty-four hours without criticizing anyone for any reason, unless human life is in danger.

If You Think It

If you think it but don't say it, does it count against your twenty-four hours?

If a critical thought enters your mind and you get rid of the thought in a moment, then it does not count and you do not have to start your twenty-four hours over. If, on the other hand, you let that critical thought stay in your mind and you develop it into a full production with quadraphonic sound and vista vision, then you must start over again.

One lady who asked this question, looked puzzled for a moment, glanced up at her husband who was standing by her side, and said, "OK. I'll try to go for twenty-four hours without criticizing or dwelling upon a critical thought."

Then, pointing to her husband, she said, "But he will never make it!" There was a pause. "Oh dear," she said, "I will have to start my twenty-four hours over again, won't I?"

"Yes," I responded. "Good luck."

In one study involving more than 800 people, after three days only twenty people had been able to go for a period of twenty-four hours without criticizing—and they had been able to count sleeping time as a part of the twenty-four hours! The responses from those who made it were interesting.

"It was easy," said one woman. "My husband and son were out of town."

One man in the group observed, "I was so criticized as a child that I decided I would not be a critical adult."

One man suggested that we form an organization called C.A. or Critaholics Anonymous and hold weekly meetings.

One mother reported that after she had gone twenty-four hours, her teenage daughter, who was unaware of her mother's efforts, asked if she were feeling OK.

Because of our culture and the accepted mode of communication, it is difficult to refrain from criticizing. We have been raised in a critical environment. We have been taught to be critical, analytical, and to subject people and things to the scientific method. Some of us have difficulty speaking a single sentence without criticizing.

Don't be too hard on yourself if you don't succeed in a week. This is a difficult assignment.

Once you master twenty-four hours, try a whole week, and when you are able to go an entire month, you will have conquered it. You may slip back into your old habit of criticizing, but you will know what you must do if you are to overcome it—start your twenty-four hours over again.

Why Should You Try?

These are the objectives you should experience by abstaining from criticism:

1. Go twenty-four hours wihout criticizing.
2. Increase your awareness of the critical nature of our society.
3. Become aware of your own compulsion to criticize.
4. Experience the power of self-mastery.

The answer to the question, "Why should I try to stop criticizing?" is simply, "So that you can lay the foundation for love and acceptance instead of rejection."

You're Still Frustrated Even Though You Don't Criticize

It is true that just because a person removes criticism, or genuinely controls it, he may not have removed the cause of frustration that motivated the criticism. Nevertheless, with criticism eliminated or under control, a vicious circle has been broken.

If you were to come into the doctor's office with a broken arm and a hangnail, you would probably want the arm set first and then the hangnail removed. So it is with criticism. First we arrest the cancer or place it in remission, and then we seek alternative ways of expressing ourselves and improving communication. In this manner, the pressure that once motivated criticism can be channeled to a more productive path.

The key to changing behavior is to build on a person's strengths instead of dwelling on his weaknesses.

When You Must Criticize

There are four basic suggestions that should be followed if criticism must be expressed:

1.   Be alone with the person.
2.   Be in emotional control.
3.   Criticize the behavior, not the person.
4.   Criticize sparingly.

Be Alone

Remember that criticism in front of others is ridiculing and belittling. When possible, arrange a time to express your concern when the two of you can be alone.

Be in Emotional Control

Railing accusations will be returned with like intensity. An honest statement on the facts, as well as your expectations will incite more consideration than emotional outburst. Crying, as a manipulative tool, will soon turn against you.

Criticize the Behavior, Not the Person

There is a world of difference in saying, "Boy, are you stupid for doing that," and saying, "You are a lot better person than that behavior indicates."

In the latter example, the behavior was separated from the person. Avoid name-calling, especially the use of such terms as "dumb," "stupid," and even more derogatory names.

Criticize Sparingly

May I suggest that you criticize so seldom that when you do use criticism you will be heard. The frequently critical person is tuned out before the message is delivered. And don't rationalize away your criticism in the name of being honest. The so-called "open" marriage, where both members feel free to express their concerns, often provides a forum for the more critical partner. Maybe the fundamental question that ought to be asked is not, "Is it honest?" but, rather, "Is it edifying, will it ultimately be uplifting, and will it be good for the relationship?"

If a criticism does not qualify under the latter, maybe it should not be raised at all.

Summary

You have been asked to do two things in this chapter:

1. Take a pledge of verbal loyalty to the relationship.
2. Go twenty-four hours without criticizing anyone for any reason.

Take the pledge as an indication of your commitment to the relationship. As a token of your willingness, stop criticizing.

Commitment and willingness are two necessary ingredients for emotional remarriage.

CHAPTER FIVE

Prime Times for Emotional Divorce

There are events, circumstances, and situations which qualify as prime times for emotional divorce. These include but are not limited to the honeymoon, the first year, employment of mothers outside of the home, arrival of the first children, departure of the last child, severe arguments, and the forties fantasy.

These critical times for emotional divorce are often associated with frustration and unmet expectations—all frustration is based on expectation. If you did not expect a clean house, you would not be frustrated by a messy one. If you did not expect a compliment, you would not be disappointed when it isn't forth coming. If you did not expect to be held, hugged, kissed, talked to, or worked for, you would not be frustrated when such things do not occur.

Buddhists believe that if you want to eliminate frustration and live in a state of complete peace, you must cease desiring. Through the eight-fold path of Buddhism, you eliminate desire for everything but internal peace. This is a marked contrast the the high achievement, goal-oriented materialism of the Western World.

As a westerner, you bring to a marriage a highly sophisticated set of conscious and subconscious expectations. Most expectations also carry value judgments: For instance, it is good to be able to enjoy leisure time, but it is bad for a man not to provide for his family.

You enter the arena of marriage filled with expectations and a belief that most of your expectations will be met. Joining you in that arena is a separate human being with a different set of expectations. You two will share some common goals, overlapping desires, and mutually shared expectations. In fact, it is not unusual to hear someone say, "I married him because we like the same things—we have so much in common."

In childhood and adolescence many of these expectations are formed by the examples of our parents—or the lack of such examples. During the dating and courtship period, a mental checklist is often subconsciously formed; however, you may find yourself attracted to someone who meets your emotional need to be accepted, but who doesn't measure up to your other expectations of a mate. Still, you may marry with the thought: "I am sure his love for me will be so great he will want to change to meet my expectations." Or you may marry with this thought: "I love him so much I will change to become whatever he needs."

The essence of maturity is the ability to distinguish between real and unreal expectations, and to adjust to a mutually satisfying relationship. Marriage sets the stage for sharing common interests and working through differences.

Experiences, in and of themselves, do not cause emotional divorce or bonding. The way we react to an experience determines whether or not it is a positive or negative one. Even loss of employment can be a positive experience for the relationship if the married couple reacts by working more closely together. On the other hand inheriting large sums of money or real estate can destroy a relationship if the marriage partners allow the affluency to separate them into unshared worlds.

It is not the experience, but the reaction to the experience that binds or divides.

The Honeymoon

The honeymoon is a critical time for emotional divorce because this is an encounter of the closest kind. Not only physical union but also emotional bonding is involved. The heart as well as the hand is extended in trust, and a total commitment to unity of purpose is initially launched.

Often, however, when these expectations are not met, one mate or the other plants the seed for emotional divorce in his heart. Euphoric acceptance and willingness to give of self begin to diminish. Fear and doubt insert themselves: Fear that one's mate will not meet his expectations, self-doubt about one's ability to measure up to the mate's desires.

These are all normal concerns. When they are expressed and discussed, they can be worked through and the honeymoon becomes even more reassuring. If they are not dealt with, the seeds of emotional divorce wait, only to blossom at a later date, and, cautiously, the careful heart begins to establish emotional defenses.

To avoid emotional divorce during the honeymoon, there must be a willingness to share insecurities about sexual performance, about having fears and doubts, about feelings of inadequacies. There must be an atmosphere wherein these concerns can be expressed without fear of being rejected, criticized, or put down.

Emotional bonding is achieved through acceptance.

The honeymoon is a time of sharing—let your goal be to give to each other. Establish the emotional goal of giving of self and each sexual encounter will be successful. Avoid setting sexual goals of climax and orgasm. Preoccupation and worry about sexual performance have been known to prevent orgasm.

Sexual objectives often become counter-productive to emotional oneness because of the undue pressure it places on one or the other partner. Inherent in any performance objective is the possibility of failure, rejection, and depression. However, by establishing an emotional objective of giving of self, the couple insures a successful experience based on a realistic expectation.

Physical delight often follows as the natural consequence of emotional sharing. The reverse is seldom true. The honeymoon is a statement to society about the importance of the husband-wife relationship. The married partners leave father and mother and form a separate unit. There is a fundamental commitment to mate that takes priority over all other relationships.

The honeymoon is a time to commit oneself to that relationship and prioritize its importance.

The First Year

The divorce rate for those married less than one year continues to be the highest. After that the rate declines sharply.

Adjustments to expectations in the areas of finances, sex, religion, in-laws, children, recreation, employment, and friends are often greater than the individuals are willing to make, in spite of the fact that they love one another.

Marriage involves compromise, sacrifice, dedication, and commitment. It involves an awareness that everyone has strengths and weaknesses. The basic question remains: "Are the weaknesses of your mate within your coping range?" That which separates those who divorce in the first year from those who do not, is not the nature of the problems they encounter, but the willingness of one or both marriage partners to work on resolving the problems.

When Children First Come

The coming of children to a home can break or bond a marriage. Reaction to pregnancy and motherhood may take the form of inexpressible joy, deep resentment, or a combination of feelings. It can also be a time of emotional divorce.

When an emotional divorce occurs at the coming of a child, it is

usually because of the wife's insensitivity to her husband's emotional needs, or because of the husband's selfishness.

The Insensitive Wife

No man can compete with a child for the attention of the mother, and win. If he demands more of her time, he is a selfish and an uncaring father. If the wife attends to her husband reluctantly, both will be resentful. Faced with this dilemma, many men withdraw emotionally. They may turn to work, sports, hobbies, athletics, friends, or to other women to find the emotional acceptance they feel themselves denied in their marriage.

It is a wise woman who recognizes this natural insecurity and makes adjustments to be sensitive to her husband.

Signs of a Sensitive Wife

She does not:

1. Use the child as a constant excuse for not going with her husband.
2. Refuse to have a babysitter in the first six months.
3. Refuse to take the child out of the house to support her husband's activities.

She will:

1. Adjust her schedule and priorities so as to make time to rest and develop some physical stamina for being a wife.
2. Compensate for lack of sexual togetherness by communicating love and acceptance in other ways.

The Selfish Husband

It is a foolish man who tries to force his wife to choose between himself and the child. If he does, he will only create resentment and often hostility towards himself.

With the child comes a responsibility to care, nurture, and provide for its well being. A wise husband will endear himself even more to his wife by practicing restraint on his needs for her time. Patience, kindness, and consideration are called for.

The process of pregnancy and childbirth extract great energy from a woman. Many feel it takes at least a full year after childbirth before a woman is physically able to cope as well as she did before pregnancy.

Signs of a Selfish Husband

1. Refuses to get up at night, even occasionally, to care for a crying child.
2. Forces his wife to choose between himself and the child.
3. Is unreasonable about his demands on his wife's time.
4. Expects his wife to do everything she did before the baby came.
5. Threatens his wife by declaring that they will have no more children.

When children come, emotional divorce can be avoided if both husband and wife are sensitive to each other's emotional needs of acceptance, appreciation, as well as the physical need for rest.

Mothers Who Work Outside of the Home

Emotional divorce does not occur by plan; it evolves gradually. Most frequently, emotional divorce occurs because of what *didn't* happen in the marriage, rather than what *did*. What was left out of the cake mix caused the problem, not faulty ingredients.

Mothers who work outside of the home face special challenges. In addition to the normal responsibilities in attending to house-

keeping and homemaking chores, mothers are expected to maintain sufficient emotional energy to be both wives and mothers. If their husbands are considerate enough to share in the homework, the burden is lighter, but nonetheless difficult.

Another real challenge faced by mothers who work outside of the home is a question of diversification; a person can be spread only so thin. Can a woman be a wife, a mother, a professional, and remain emotionally married? It depends on the woman. Some women work to maintain emotional balance. Working outside of the home gives them a perspective they claim they would not otherwise have. Conversely, there are many who feel guilty as they drop their children off at the day-care center, and resent their husbands who insist that they work. Homes can survive two working spouses and maintain emotional bonding if each partner is dedicated to the cause of creating a supportive home environment. However, when both spouses work outside of the home, it increases the probability of emotional divorce, even with practical consideration in saving time and emotional energy.

Many mothers who work outside of the home run the risk of an extramarital affair with an understanding man they might meet in the business world. Mothers who work at home seem less inclined to extramarital affairs because they lack the contact with men which is experienced daily in the business world.

Two recommendations are offered to couples who deem it necessary that both husband and wife be employed outside of the home:

1. Hire part-time help to assist in house-cleaning chores. Husbands as well as wives claim it is the best money they spend. The psychological as well as physical uplift it brings is often the difference between coping and not coping with the combined pressures.
2. A weekly date is also important. The date does not focus on spending money, but spending time in feeling-level activities,

such as touching, talking, sharing. This is a commitment to the relationship, an acknowledgement that the relationship is separate from all other relationships.

Empty Nest Syndrome

Around the time (either before or after) the youngest child prepares to graduate from high school, divorce is a common phenomenon. So frequent is the occurance of divorce at this time that family therapists refer to it as the "empty nest" syndrome.

It is not so much a critical time for emotional divorce, as it is a symptom that emotional divorce has happened years earlier, and one mate or the other stayed in the marriage "for the sake of the children." Few instances are as dramatic as the following story related by a surprised wife:

> It was graduation night. The last of our four children was graduating from high school. We came home from the program, our daughter opened her graduation gift, and my husband called me into the kitchen and announced he had fulfilled his obligation to me and to the children. His camper was packed and he was leaving. He left just like that. Later I heard from his attorney about the divorce. Thirty-two years we were married, but he walked out. We had our fights and quarrels just like everybody, but I can honestly say I did not have the slightest clue he would ever leave. He was a fine father and a good provider. I still cannot believe he is gone.

As the history of this case began to filter in, the pattern of emotional divorce took shape.

When children came to the marriage and demanded more and more of the mother's time, the husband asserted his emotional needs only to be rejected in the name of motherhood. Over the years, he burned out in his affection for his wife, and emotionally divorced her. He diverted his attention, for emotional reinforcement, to his children and became deeply involved in hunting and fishing and in his job.

She, on the other hand, found total fulfillment in the progress of their children. She was, by all standards, a devoted mother. Nevertheless, she found herself facing the greatest trauma of her life, alone.

Her great test was not divorce, but the fact that her last child was leaving home. Her identity, self-concept, and, most important, her emotional needs were all wrapped up in the marriages of her children, and she had already been accused of being a problem mother-in-law.

We talked about her compulsion to call her children every day and involve herself in their marriages. I explained to her that when an individual has all of her emotional cookies wrapped up in a single bag, it is understandable that she would have such a difficult time letting go. I warned her, however, that if she did not begin to rediscover herself as an individual, all of her years of dedicated motherhood would be repaid by her children in the form of resentment, hostility, and rejection.

"But I don't know how to stop caring," she said as she cried.

"I'm not asking you to stop caring, and neither are your children. You can care without calling them every day on the phone. Be available to them, but not over-involved.

"The key is to redirect your life to productive pursuits. You need to find additional activities that will meet your emotional needs of acceptance, appreciation, and giving of self. There are a great many important and worthwhile causes that need your support. There are church and community groups that would welcome your involvement. Schools and hospitals and nursing homes are always ready for a willing worker.

"You may want to think about returning to school to complete your formal education. There are a number of other classes you may want to take just because you are interested. The local community college sponsors a variety of classes in adult education ranging from pottery making to weather forecasting.

"You need to be involved in activities outside of the lives of your children. Can you see that in one way it is selfish of you to be so involved in all they do? You are not doing it just for them, you are doing it to meet your own needs.

"Your children love you, but you must be sensitive at this point in your life not to use their love, or subconsciously manipulate them. You might create problems in their marriages if you force your children to choose between you and their mates. In addition, you will probably succeed in making them feel guilty that they do not respond to your desires."

Looking back at this woman's life, we see the time when her husband was asserting his emotional needs. At this time we would not encourage her to be less of a mother, but both a great mother and a great wife. This was a classic case, unfortunately, for she was a great mother and a lousy wife.

If she had learned not to use motherhood as an excuse for abandoning her role as a wife, she would still have her husband's support. Instead, her need for her children is intensified by his absence.

This tragedy need not have occurred. She needed to have been more sensitive to his needs, and remember that before she was a mother, she was a mate. After her children had gone, she could have continued to be a mate, but as it is, she joins the ranks of hundreds of women who are alone.

Severe Arguments

A severe argument which leads to emotional divorce is one in which feelings are hurt and deep wounds are made, not necessarily one accompanied by yelling and screaming.

Many severe arguments are quiet conversations that nevertheless leave one or both partners emotionally devastated. Such arguments are attacks upon the self-concept, attacks that criticize, that maim and destroy, that reject and tear down the self-worth of a spouse.

It is a myth that blowing up and then getting over it is healthy for a relationship. One may feel better temporarily, but the relationship will suffer serious damage. There are more productive ways of expressing anger and frustration than by emotionally attacking a loved one.

Two problems must be considered. One is *the issue that is the cause of the upset,* and the other is *the anger or frustration associated with it.*

Most issues can be handled without destroying the self-concept. Many couples work out a system to resolve conflict by agreeing to set a special time for discussing it. Some write it out in a letter. Some agree not to attack the person, but to deal with the issue, some propose at least one solution for every problem, etc. Severe arguments are not necessary, and in fact they can be avoided if a pattern for resolving conflict can be agreed upon.

The second issue, that of what to do with anger, has age-old remedies: go for a walk, take a cold shower, jog a mile, count to ten, buy a punching bag, or knit ten rows on an afghan. But do not turn your verbal aggression on your mate, for after your tirade is over and you make up, you will find there is always more emotional blood spilled than you can replace. The cumulative effect of such tirades will be emotional divorce.

The Forties Fantasy

Many couples feel estrangement during the period known as middle age, a time of great insecurity for many. Basic questions surface: Am I loved and accepted? Am I appreciated? Do I feel a sense of belonging? Am I valued in my employment? Does anyone recognize the contributions I have made, or see my potential for an even greater contribution?

Men and women question their ability to be loved as they see younger men and women beginning to excel and surpass them in talent, beauty, and ability. They realize that youth has forever fled, their bodies begin to react to age, and in a desperate grasp to recapture the vitality of youth, they launch forth on elaborate physical fitness programs, diets, and often set out in quest of materialistic symbols of security.

Bill, for example, was a successful lawyer, 42 years old and mostly bald. Many thought him to be much older. One day he came home in the afternoon and told his wife that he wanted a toupee.

"You don't need a toupee," she said with a laugh, "I like you just the way you are."

Nevertheless, he purchased a very expensive toupee, started jogging, and bought a membership in a racquet ball club.

His wife was bewildered by his behavior, but this was only the beginning.

Next he bought a sports car and a new wardrobe. His children were stunned, but supportive. His wife reacted by withdrawing. She was comfortable with her home, friends, family, and, she thought, with her husband. But soon he wanted her to change. "Let's take up tennis," he suggested.

"Go ahead without me," she encouraged.

He did and began playing three or four days a week. Then one morning he said to his wife, "Before I die and leave all that I have accumulated to you and the children, I want to travel and see the world. Let's go to Europe. What do you say?"

Reluctantly she went but in her mind she began to question whether she really knew him. Soon his demands on her time became unreasonable from her point of view.

The following spring he bought bicycles for the entire family and proposed a 50-mile trip.

"You and the kids go ahead," she said.

By summer he was involved wih a girl 18 years younger than

himself, and by fall he was divorced from his wife and married to the girl, who was only three years older than his oldest child.

The foregoing story, with a thousand variations, is repeated daily, but the prevention for such cases is simple. There are basic needs for acceptance, love, belonging, togetherness, appreciation, praise, recognition, and giving of self. A wise and sensitive mate does not let her husband "go on ahead without her." Instead, she rides out the storm of insecurity—which will pass—and their relationship survives.

Karen was 43, the mother of three children, and deeply distressed about passing through early menopause. Her husband was hard-working, quiet, and quite a homebody. She worked as a secretary for a construction firm. Everything in her life was routine, and she felt trapped by her circumstances. The pressures of being a wife, a homemaker, a cook, and house cleaner every Saturday were getting to her. Her job was just that, a job—a way to make a few dollars that never seemed to be enough. She went home tired every night and faced children who would not clean up after themselves. Their rooms were always a mess, they listened to insane music, and they talked back. They wanted money, the car, and total freedom without responsibility. Karen was in a syndrome where she *gave*, and everybody else *took*.

One day at the office, a subcontractor, a good-looking man about 38, paid her a sincere compliment on her work. She was astounded. It was the first time in a long while that anybody had expressed appreciation to her for anything.

Over a period of weeks, they chatted in friendly conversation. Then one day he said to her, "I want to be with you."

Her face flushed, and before she thought, she had said, "I know; I want to be with you, too."

For the next several months they met in parking lots and had various rendezvous. He was divorced and madly in love with her and wanted her to divorce and marry him.

She lived in two worlds. Occasionally, she was caught in a lie. Finally, she couldn't take the duplicity any longer and confessed the whole thing to her husband and asked for a divorce. Family, friends, and relatives were devastated, but she divorced anyway.

This is not the story of a sexually deprived wife. Nevertheless, she was emotionally hungry and, frankly, emotionally neglected. Though she loved her husband and children, she received very little from them in terms of emotional support, and found herself giving and giving and giving with nothing coming back to her. Emotionally speaking, she was a prime target for an affair. She was flattered that a younger man found her attractive and wanted her. She was even more impressed that he wanted to give to her; to give her his time, to talk to her, to give her presents, to care about what she thought and what she said.

Her husband wasn't abusive to her, and when the divorce came, he was overwhelmed and incredulous, but her need for appreciation was greater than her need to "act responsibly."

"I didn't know," said the husband. "What did I do wrong?"

Again, it wasn't what he did; it was his insensitivity to his wife's needs, and his lack of knowledge of how to fulfill the need, had he recognized it. Ignorance and insensitivity are excuses that bring no consolation to a broken home.

When people are hungry, they are often fussy about what they eat, but when a person is starving, he will eat things he never thought possible. The same principle applies to emotional starvation. Hungry people are picky; starving people aren't.

How could she leave her family? Simple. She was starving, and no one noticed.

Summary

When a person is emotionally starving the period is critical. There are certain circumstances that occur with such frequency that emotional divorce is predictable. The honeymoon, the first year, the coming of children, the mother who works outside the home, severe arguments, the empty nest syndrome, and the forties fantasy, are circumstances that may open the way to emotional divorce. The remedy for these prime times of emotional divorce is an extra dose of awareness and sensitivity and a willingness to be accepting, caring, and appreciative.

CHAPTER SIX

Learning the Love Language of Your Mate

We learn to communicate love and acceptance in different ways. One key to avoiding emotional divorce, or to establishing or re-establishing emotional bonding, is to learn your mate's love language.

Take the following quiz. Be honest and respond as you truly feel. There are no wrong answers. The right answers are the ones you give.

Love Language Quiz

Choose only one answer per set of questions, even though more than one may apply. These questions pertain to you as a child, as a parent, or as a spouse.

1. What statement best describes you?

    a.   Physically expressive
    b.   Verbally expressive
    c.   Goal oriented

2. As a child I received

    a. Hugs and kisses
    b. Verbal praise
    c. Gifts and presents

3. My family demonstrated love

    a. By touching
    b. By telling each other
    c. It was just understood

4. In communicating affection to my mate, I prefer to give

    a. Tender kisses
    b. Tender words
    c. A gift of tender meaning

5. I would most enjoy receiving from my companion

    a. A hug and a kiss when we meet in the evening
    b. A phone call during the day
    c. A surprise note expressing appreciation

6. I would rather have my mate

    a. Be physically expressive and loving
    b. Recognize my efforts with words of appreciation
    c. Repair a small thing like a screen door, or mend a pair of pants.

7. For a gift, I would most enjoy

    a. A coupon that said, "Good for one month of good morning kisses"
    b. A personal, handwritten love letter
    c. My favorite home cooked meal or dinner at a nice restaurant

8. I would prefer

    a. A night on the town and a late-night dinner for two
    b. To have my mate pay me a compliment in the company of friends, family, or just when we're alone
    c. Help with the dishes, trimming the lawn, or work with me on some project

9. I would prefer

    a. A kiss
    b. The words, "I love you"
    c. A small gift

10. I would prefer

    a. A romantic weekend
    b. A long heart-to-heart talk
    c. A clean house or well-kept yard

11. It is more important to have my mate

    a. Sit close to me in the car
    b. Talk to me about the day's events
    c. Remember to run an errand for me

12. I would rather

    a. Be embraced and treated romantically
    b. Be told I'm loved
    c. Be shown, by hard work, that I'm loved

13. I would prefer to have my mate

    a. Reach out and touch me
    b. Say, "I love you"
    c. Surprise me with a good deed

14.   I would prefer giving

    a.   An embrace
    b.   A kind word
    c.   Flowers

15.   With which of these statements do you most agree?

    a.   I would rather hold hands in public, or walk arm-in-arm, and mean it, than live in a fancy house.
    b.   I would rather be told I was loved, than be married to a workaholic who is always giving me everything but him/herself.
    c.   You shouldn't have to tell somebody you love them all the time; they should know it by the way they are treated.

16.   I most agree that

    a.   Just being held can be emotionally satisfying.
    b.   You cannot know a person unless you really talk to him.
    c.   There is a time and a place for everything—showing affection in public makes me nervous.

17.   I prefer expressing appreciation by

    a.   A pat on the back
    b.   A phone call
    c.   Sending a note

18.   As a reward for "good grades," I would give

    a.   Some physical expression
    b.   Some praise
    c.   Some money

19.   I would be most inclined to criticize a teenager for

    a.   Not being respectful of their parents' wishes
    b.   Not being appreciative of what they have
    c.   Not keeping their room clean

20. As a parent, I would be more inclined to
     a. Spank
     b. Scold
     c. Make the child sit in a corner

21. If I enjoyed dancing, I would do so because of the
     a. Physical closeness
     b. Social interaction
     c. Physical exercise

22. As a parent of a young child, I would prefer
     a. Playing games
     b. Reading to them
     c. Going for a walk

23. Basically I am
     a. Romantic
     b. Talkative
     c. Hard working

Total number of A answers ____, B answers ____, C answers ____

A = touch-oriented   B = verbal-oriented   C = task-oriented

Your primary love language is your highest score. Your secondary love language is your second highest score.

If a person were clearly a "touch-," or "verbal-," or "task-oriented" person, it would be easier to learn his love language. Many of us are a combination of these, although one will tend to emerge as a dominant characteristic of a person's love language.

It becomes important to understand your spouse's love language, and to communicate with him in that language. It is unreasonable and unproductive to expect him to change his love language. It is not unreasonable, however, to expect him to understand your language and to communicate to you in that language.

Whether your spouse is a touch-oriented person, a verbally-oriented person, or a task-oriented person, learn his language and accept as sacred his offering of love to you. This is empathy. Learn also to return his love in such a manner that he can appreciate it. Love language is a key to avoiding emotional divorce, and is essential to emotional remarriage.

Love Language Defined

A person's love language is defined by the way he sends and receives messages of acceptance, affection and appreciation. It is much broader than a sexual expression for it encompasses the total range of caring responses. It is how you say, "I love you, I accept you, and I appreciate you."

The Eye, the Ear, the Hand

Task-centered people often define their values in terms of accomplishments. It is what the eye can see. Achievement is very important. Hard work, status, or things often become the measures of their self-worth.

Verbally-oriented people are excited about sharing their feelings. Talking and listening remain paramount. The ear and the mouth are the focus. Heart-to-heart talks, caring words, and meaningful discussions comprise the love language of the verbally-centered.

Touch-oriented people enjoy the complete range of physical expression. The hand symbolizes all touching experiences. Holding hands, hugging, and being physically close communicate love.

The Golden Rule, With a Twist

An interesting twist to the golden rule applies to learning your mate's love language. Your mate will treat you the way he wants to be treated by you when communicating messages of love, acceptance, and appreciation. It is a wise person who can perceive his mate's love language and respond to it.

Decoding Your Mates Love Language

Decoding your mate's love language requires an understanding of his primary medium of "feeling level" communication. Is he touch-, task-, or verbally-centered? What does it mean to your mate to love and to be loved in return? How does he interpret caring responses?

Love language is both a reflection of and a reaction to the emotional climate of youth. Love language was mostly learned in the home when you were a child and an adolescent. Since it was learned, it can be changed if we choose to do so. Because of the power of will, human beings are capable of profound change and adjustment. However, most relationships do not demand profound change as much as they require understanding.

Some marriage partners come from homes that are very touch-oriented; that is, there was a lot of hugging, kissing, and touching between their father and mother, or between one of their parents and the children. Love and acceptance were communicated by some physical expression. For example, when the child brought home a good report card, the mother would pick up the child and give him or her a big hug. Multiply that experience a few hundred times and it is easy to understand why many marriage partners interpret touching as acceptance.

Picture for a moment the same child returning home with a good report card to a family that was not touch-oriented, but verbally-supportive.

"I'm very proud of you," the mother might say. "You are a wonderful example to your brothers and sisters."

Multiply that experience a few hundred times and it becomes clear why many feel the need to be told—verbally—that they are loved.

Assume that the same child came home to a family which was neither touch-oriented nor verbally-active, but where it was simply understood that you were loved and people would show their love by the "things" they do for each other. In such a home environment, you would be more likely to receive money as a reward for good grades than a hug or verbal praise. Love and acceptance would be demonstrated by working hard for the loved ones, by providing "things" for them—what you did *for* them, not *to* them, would communicate love and acceptance. Multiply these experiences a few hundred times and you begin to understand why some people prefer having dinner on time to being told, "I love you."

It would be an oversimplification to state that we simply reflect our home environment. There are many additional factors which affect our orientation to task, touch, or verbal communication. The home remains, however, the seed bed from which we grow.

In general, task-centered people are influenced by task-centered parents, etc. It is possible, though, to have touch, task, and verbal children all coming from the same home. As the individual reacts with family, friends, and peers, their emotional needs will incline them to touch-, task-, or verbal-orientation.

In a Crisis

One's disposition to be touch-, task-, or verbally-centered in general is often altered by the crisis of a specific challenge. For example, under the threat of financial disaster a touch-oriented person may become quite task-centered in order to survive the pending fiscal catastrophe. Once the crisis is over, however, he will often revert to his previous orientation of being touch-, task- or verbally-centered.

In the subsequent chapters, verbal-, task-, and touch-orientations will be dealt with in greater detail. You may think you are oriented one way, only to find out that you feel differently under certain circumstances.

CHAPTER SEVEN

Learning the Love Language of the Verbally-Oriented Person

A verbally-oriented marriage partner is one who places great value on the word as a primary channel for communicating love, acceptance, and appreciation. Nevertheless, verbally-centered mates do not necessarily talk a lot. In fact, it is quite possible to be verbally-oriented and thought of as a "quiet type." Most talkative people, however, are verbally-oriented, not so much on the quantity of their words, as upon the quality of the caring words they use or need.

Frequency of Caring Words

A non-verbal spouse would do well to think of "caring words" as "food" for his mate. If you eat or dine only once a month, your relationship will starve to death if you are verbally-centered.

Sometimes a family therapist will hear the non-verbal mate ask: "Why do I always have to tell him that I love him? He should know it by how I treat him, by how hard I work, and by the fact that we've been married for 30 years. I know he loves me, I don't have to be told every day that I am loved. I think he is insecure and immature and needs to grow up."

Insecure? Perhaps. Immature? Not necessarily. Each of us has our security blanket. It may not be verbal or tactile; it might be material possessions, God, or a strong self-concept. Whatever it is, take our security blanket away and see how quickly we become insecure.

It is relatively painless to be thoughtful and to care enough to communicate frequently, even to daily share your "bread" with a loved one who is verbally-oriented by saying, "I love you."

In one situation a frustrated woman who was very verbally-centered, destroyed a mink coat. It was her husband's gift to her for their 25th wedding anniversary.

"I have told you a thousand times," she said, throwing the coat at him, "I don't want things from you. I want you to tell me that you love me. In twenty-five years you have only told me that you loved me five times."

Incredible as it may sound, she named the five dates, including the day, the month, and the year.

"I admit it," said the husband, "I am a quiet man. It embarrasses me to talk about loving someone. In my home, as we were growing up, I knew I was loved. Nobody had to tell me all the time. It was just understood. My wife and I live in an exclusive part of town, she has a maid, and everything she wants. I am always giving her gifts. How can she question my love?"

The Art of Translation

In counsel the verbally-oriented woman from the foregoing example had to learn the art of translation. For example, translate your husband's task-oriented disposition into verbal communication. Every time your husband gives you something, repeat out loud or in your mind, "I have just been told that I am loved," and react the same way you would have reacted if he had actually said, "I love you." In his love language, that is precisely what he has done. Don't demand that he say, "I love you." In a way you are demanding that everyone in France speak English just because you speak English.

She accepted the assignment of going home to practice "translating" for the next two weeks, but when she returned, she confessed only a half-hearted effort.

The husband was advised, "Don't cop out by saying, 'That's the way I am and there is nothing I can do about it.' Continue to give gifts because it pleases you. Also, be willing to say, 'I love you.' If it embarrasses you to say it in front of the children, then take your wife off to a private corner every day and tell her you love her. Go home and try it for two weeks." He also returned and admitted that he had not really tried.

There was nothing more their counselor could do. Their mutual stubbornness defied solution.

The tragedy of this situation was their reluctance to understand and accept each other's love language. They were unwilling to make any efforts to communicate in one another's language, demanding instead that their spouse understand them. This particular marriage ended in divorce, but there were solutions to this couple's problems. Unwillingness, however, defeated all the solutions.

Kim, on the other hand, was a verbally-active twenty-six-year-old who was married to a strong, silent type. Her husband was content with the marriage, but Kim was depressed much of the time. She expected to be told daily that she was loved, just as her mother had been told by her father.

The counselor talked to Kim about the art of translating, and she was eager to try and fascinated by the idea. "How does your husband tell you he loves you?" she was asked.

"By being a good provider," she replied.

"Every time he leaves for work this next month, say to yourself, 'Thank you for telling me you love me by how hard you work.'"

After a month, her depression had fled because her expectation had been met by learning the art of translation.

A Verbally Active Person is Often His Own Therapist

Most verbally active people have a greater need for someone to listen to them than to talk to them. They are looking for sounding boards. Frequently, the need to talk through each alternative, even though their non-verbal, or perhaps their impatiently verbal mate might already have the solution to the problem. Many people need to talk over each alternative to satisfy themselves that their decisions are sound, and when they are cut off, they are frustrated.

It requires patience on the part of the mate to listen and practice the art of receiving: Focusing on the message, giving 100% attention to the messenger, being sincere, and showing that he understands. He should question if he doesn't understand. A verbally-active person is often his own therapist, and he works through his problems and insecurities if he has someone who will listen.

The Art of Listening

One of the best ways to develop the art of listening is to develop your ability to keep others talking. Just being quiet is not sufficient, though it is important to know when to be quiet.

"Why," you ask, "is it important to keep someone else talking?"

Research indicates that people who are encouraged to verbalize begin, in a matter of minutes, to give positive, feeling-level responses.

Many therapists have learned that silence, even an awkward uncomfortableness, leads the counselee to begin to talk. Often the preliminary conversation is flack, but if the counselee continues to verbalize, he quickly exhausts the superficial and begins to reach a positive feeling level. If he is cut off or side-tracked, he may never reach the level of positive feeling.

Why is it important to reach a level of positive feeling? Unless such a level is reached in a relationship, you may never deal with the real issues.

A World of Flack

The following story illustrates how easy it is to dwell in a world of flack and never deal with the "gut issues."

Consider the case of Phil.

Phil arises every morning at 5:00 a.m. to commence a vigorous program of jogging and exercise. On the particular morning in question, he returns at 6:00 a.m. to shower and shave. On the way to the bathroom, he strikes his little toe on the end of the bed. He was walking in full stride, and the pain is tremendous. He may have even broken the toe. There is a cut, some bleeding, and his toe throbs as he limps toward the bathroom.

Arriving at the bathroom, he discovers it is occupied. "Who is in there?" he yells.

The sound of the blow dryer and the voice which responds confirms that it is his teen-age daughter.

"Well, get out of there," Phil shouts. "You're always in the bathroom. Something must be wrong with you. Nobody needs to spend that much time in a bathroom blow-drying their hair."

"You're always yelling at me," says the daughter as she exits in tears.

The daughter, now upset, goes downstairs for breakfast. Her mother is turning pancakes, contentedly thinking about the day's activities. The daughter enters the kitchen and says, "We *always* have pancakes."

"Well," retorts the mother, jarred out of her reverie, "if you don't like my pancakes, you can go without breakfast!"

"I'd rather go without breakfast than have to eat pancakes!" rejoins the daughter.

"That's fine with me," says the mother, and the daughter stomps out of the room, slams the door, and marches to the bus stop even more upset.

Now the mother is upset, the daughter is upset, and Phil is limping down the stairs on his way to breakfast. He likes pancakes, but entering the kitchen, he declares, "That daughter of yours is always in the bathroom."

His wife slaps three pancakes on a plate, sets the plate firmly on the table, and says, "So what!"

Phil, his toe still throbbing, goes into a tirade which eventually winds up in an argument. His wife leaves the kitchen in tears, and Phil goes off to work suffering from frustration—not to mention pain.

This entire episode would be comical if it weren't so emotionally devastating to everyone involved. These are the real issues: Phil's injured toe, his wife's feeling of being unappreciated, and his daughter's feeling of being rejected. None of the real issues were even dealt with. The entire event concerned itself with negative verbal flack.

Many people live day after day in a world of verbal flack, and never get to the level of positive feeling or deal with real issues.

Keep Someone Talking

The ability, or the skill, to reach the level of positive feeling is developed through the art of active listening. It is important to a verbally as well as to a non-verbally-oriented person to be able to develop this ability. The essence of communication in marriage is to be able to express and communicate feelings and to allow others to do so.

As a measure of your ability to be an active listener, see how long you can keep someone talking. As an assignment (an experiment) select someone—a friend, a relative, or a total stranger—and, using your basic listening skills, see how long you can keep him talking. Do not pick someone who is so verbally active that all you have to do is call on the phone and say, "Hi," and he will talk for two hours. And remember, the object is for him to talk and for you to encourage him, so, obviously, you will have to say something.

Here are some suggestions:

Active Listening Skills

1. Ask questions that cannot be answered with a "yes," or a "no," or with a single word. For example, "Where are you from?" can be answered by saying, "Denver," and that's the end of conversation. "Are you here for a long stay?" may be answered with a "yes" or a "no." These kinds of questions do not stimulate thinking or positive feeling level communication. Such polite convertation has its place, and it may break the ice with a verbally active person, but questions to ask are those which will stimulate thinking: "What do you think?" "What is your opinion?" "How do you feel about—?" "Why do you feel—?" "Why do you imagine they would do that?" "What are you going to do now?" "How did all this happen?" It is difficult to answer these questions with a "yes," a "no," or a single word.

2. Nod your head if you understand what he is saying, or ask him to explain if you don't. If you agree with what is being said, encourage him by adding one-, or two-word comments such as "That's true," "I agree," or "Isn't that the case?"

3. Appropriate eye contact is helpful in developing the art of active listening, but staring at someone is considered impolite. In fact, staring without moving your head is a body language signal often interpreted as hostility, disagreement, or resistance. If you want to stimulate and encourage conversation, especially on a positive-feeling level, you need

appropriate eye contact. Interrupt occasionally with a direct question such as, "What do you mean?" and look at the person. When he responds maintain eye contact and nod your head. Many verbally-active people as well as active listeners have developed these skills as a natural part of their lives. Others have to practice them until they become natural.

4. Do not fold your arms or cross your legs or lean back when someone is talking to you. These are all non-verbal turnoffs. Subconsciously, the folding of our arms acts as a barrier between yourself and the message of the person talking. It may mean he is discussing something that has struck a sensitive nerve with you or that you are resisting the message. Leaning back is withdrawal. Crossing your legs is frequently a defense mechanism or a way of showing disinterest.

5. Don't stand or sit too close to the person. This often is interpreted as a violation of a person's personal space, and anything closer than arm's length may carry sexual overtones.

6. Lean slightly forward when sitting, clasp your hands, and let them rest in your lap. This sign of openness creates an environment which encourages the expression of feelings.

7. If you are standing, face the person and let your arms rest at your sides. This promotes openness.

8. Touching your face with your hand from time to time indicates contemplation, thought, and meditation.

9. Both facial expression and tone of voice are very important in communication. One psychologist claims that people react to what is said on the following basis:

    55% to facial expression
    38% to tone of voice
    7% to choice of words

Even pets, especially dogs and cats, learn to read the facial expressions of their masters and to react to the tone of their master's voice. Little children also respond to tone of voice.

Adults are somewhat more sophisticated; they do not always mean what they say, either in tone or in choice of words. There is an element of trust, however, extended to loved ones. You are judged to be sincere until there is evidence to the contrary. Both facial expression and tone of voice are important elements in the quality of your verbal ability.

10. Be honest and sincere. Without these necessary ingredients, active listening is meaningless in achieving a level of positive feeling.

Reaching a Positive-Feeling Level

While studying for a Master's degree at the University of Washington, I was assigned to go home and see how long I could keep my wife talking. The instructions indicated I should use all the verbal and non-verbal skills in my possession.

I went forth, armed with my new-found skills, ready and anxious to engage in an exciting adventure. It was about 4:30 p.m. when I arrived home. The children had already returned from school, and my wife was in the kitchen preparing the evening meal.

After some small talk about the day, I leaned across the counter, looked intently at her, and began asking her thought provoking questions. At first she looked surprised. Quickly, however, she began to express her thoughts. I nodded my head, maintained appropriate eye contact, and interrupted occasionally to have her expand on a feeling or an idea.

I soon discovered I had a tiger by the tail. Once she began expressing herself and reached the feeling level, she moved to sharing some of her innermost desires, frustrations, and concerns. The flood gates were opened and a veritable ocean of feelings came pouring through. The noise of the children faded into the background, and two-and-a-half hours later, I collapsed, emotionally drained, but she seemed to be getting stronger, her mind more invigorated. Then, as she finished the one-sided conversation, she said something that was both humorous and instructive: "That was the best conversation we've had in a long time."

From this experience, and from sixteen years of marriage and family counseling, I have learned to be careful when dealing with human expression. There are many times that it would not be productive to open up feeling-level communication. The "right time" and the "right place" are not just cliches, but realities. Quite often, when people open up their feelings, they fear they have said too much and they subsequently try to avoid you. You may also feel uncomfortable about what is said. When that happens, you need to have the courage to cut them off, or to stop and assure them that you will keep their confidences.

With husbands and wives, it is important to be able to express your innermost thoughts, feelings, and fears, and know that you will not be rejected. The greatest need one feels in the husband-wife relationship is the need to be accepted. Shortcomings, faults, and failings cause us to seek the answer to the question Tevye posed to his wife in *Fiddler on the Roof*: "Do you love me?" In other words, "Do you accept me? In spite of all my fears and faults will you stay with me? If I am totally revealed to you, can I trust you to love me and care for me?"

It becomes obvious that if we are to avoid emotional divorce, we need to stay emotionally married. This does not mean that we dwell on the emotional level all of the time, but it does mean that when occasions arise which require a positive, feeling-level communication, we are capable of reaching into our bag of active listening skills and creating the environment that will produce meaningful interaction.

A Time for Talk

It is often difficult for a non-verbal person to understand the importance of talking to a verbally-centered mate. The verbally-active individual is often perceived as a chipmunk whose endless chatter is a source of irritation. If emotional divorce is to be avoided, a regular commitment of quality time is essential to insure communication and to meet the need of the verbally-oriented companion.

The prescription is simple, yet it requires commitment and diligence: Date once a week for the rest of your lives.

Courting and dating were most likely the very things that brought you to the point of making a marriage commitment. During that dating and courting period there was considerable sharing of feelings, desires, dreams, and hopes. Verbal interaction played an important role in the growth of your relationship.

Too often the wedding altar marks the end of courtship instead of the beginning of a special courtship intended to last a lifetime. The idea of continuing an attitude of courtship after marriage requires getting out the calendar and planning on specific occasions when the two of you can go on a date. Those who just let things happen will find themselves controlled by circumstances and bound by the calendars of others.

A weekly date does not have to be an exotic affair. The focus is not on the event, but on the purpose of a weekly date—to communicate. Going to a movie, a party or a dance is not as important as the verbal interchange and the attitude which surrounds that particular activity. Again, the focus is not on spending money, but on spending time, quality time, and spending it in positive communication. The conversation which takes place going to or coming from an activity is probably more important to the verbally-centered mate than the activity itself.

Going out together does not guarantee good communication, but at least it creates a special setting where communication can occur. It fosters a positive environment and a climate conducive to reinforcing your basic commitment to one another. Avoid dating situations where you are always together with another couple. The idea is for the two of you to re-establish your relationship as husband and wife. Frequently (at least twice a month) the date should involve just the two of you.

A date doesn't require a great expense. Many times, for young marrieds, it is impossible to afford anything—including a babysitter. Just remember that it is the commitment to dating and to a weekly time together that is important. If necessary, trade baby tending with another young couple in order to go on a walk for your date. Once a couple makes a commitment to this principle of dating once a week—every week for the rest of their lives—ways and means will be found to adhere to the principle.

This weekly time commitment can become one of the most meaningful parts of your life. Notice also that both the husband and the wife must be committed to this dating concept if it is going to accomplish its purpose.

It is never too late to start dating as a married couple. Remember, people grow in love and out of love several times in the course of the same marriage. A seventy-four-year-old man laughed at the idea of dating his seventy-two-year-old wife once a week. "That's my problem now," he explained, "I'm with her all the time."

"Yes," I responded, "but it has been a while since you really talked."

He reluctantly accepted the assignment, and after three months of weekly dating, he returned to say, "I think I'll keep her!"

You cannot continue to ignore the husband-wife relationship without experiencing the natural consequences of emotional divorce. Dating on a weekly basis is not the whole answer, merely part of the attempt to say that the marriage relationship is worth separate time. Watching TV together is not enough; not even just being together all day long is enough. It must be quality time.

It may well be that a quality weekly date could be the only time the two of you completely share. People's lives have a way of becoming immensely complex, and avoiding emotional divorce requires you to do something positive together.

Living together does not guarantee communication any more than dating does, unless it is understood that the purpose for the date is to share feelings. Occasionally the date may consist of "clearing the air," but this can often be done without a date. The primary purpose for the date is to positively reinforce the relationship. Therefore, avoid the temptation of using the date as an opportunity to vent your frustrations. On rare occasions, "let it all hang out," but in the main, the date should be planned so that it is an edifying experience.

How Important Is This Weekly Date?

For years, a weekly date has been a part of my relationship with my wife. The date may be a lunch together or an event in which we observe one of the children performing, but it has become an institution, something the children expect and support.

On one occasion, very special to our relationship, and one for which my wife purchased a new dress and made an appointment with the hairdresser, we were interrupted by a phone call just as we were ready to leave. A friend of the family called to ask if I would go to the hospital because his aging mother was dying, and he wanted my moral support. I talked it over with my wife, who willingly sacrificed her evening for this exceptional situation.

We postponed our special date just one day and so the next day we planned for it as we had the previous day. My wife was a vision of loveliness as we prepared to leave, but once again, the phone rang. It was my friend. His mother had not passed away, but she was failing rapidly—could I please come up and help him through this experience?

I explained that I could not, called a mutual friend, and he agreed that he would spend the night in the hospital with our friend, whose mother died that night.

We are still friends, and I am still married, and, more important, emotionally married. You can only bump the husband-wife relationship so many times until the natural consequences of emotional divorce overtake one or both of the married partners. To some, it is incomprehensible that a date with one's wife could be more important than helping a friend through a crisis, but if we are not very careful, we find friends, family, children, in-laws, employment, and personal recreation all becoming more important than a date with our husband or wife.

Reasonable flexibility is certainly necessary, but if you change the date every week, that in itself is a commentary on the commitment to the relationship. When almost anything becomes a good reason to cancel the date, it is time to check the pulse of the marriage.

Suggestions for Meeting Needs of the Verbally-Oriented Mate

1. A phone call, however brief, and the words, "I love you," are especially appreciated by the verbally-centered mate.
2. Notes, poems, and, once a year, a handwritten love letter speak to their soul.
3. A card with a coupon in it that reads: "Good for one heart-to-heart talk. You pick the time and place."
4. If you give a gift or reach out to touch your mate, accompany it with caring words.
5. Make it a practice to compliment your mate in the company of friends, family, or when the two of you are alone.
6. When you meet in the evening, always ask about the day's events, and then practice active listening. It doesn't need to take long.
7. Occasionally ask this question, "Do we need to talk?"
8. Remember to say, "I love you," every time you part company for work, to go to the store, or for an extended period of time. The words will linger in his/her mind.
9. Should a day go by without the verbally-centered mate hearing the words, "I love you," put a reminder on a calendar

and tell them so each day for thirty days. If you miss a day, start your thirty days over.

10. Send a cassette tape of your recitation of a favorite love poem such as "How Do I Love Thee, Let Me Count the Ways," etc. You may need to go to the library to do some research.

Some may think these things a bit corny and unnecessary, but it is interesting to note how many "corny" people are still emotionally married while their sophisticated counterparts struggle with emotional divorce.

Verbal Exercise: Talk to Me

How do you verbally express:

Acceptance

Affection

Appreciation

1. Without using the word "acceptance," tell your mate that you accept him/her.
2. Without using the word "affection," describe your caring feelings.
3. Without using the word "appreciation," verbally express your appreciation for your mate.

Remember, it takes practice to improve in any skill. To express caring feelings is a skill which is a combination of emotional sincerity and the use of appropriately chosen words.

CHAPTER EIGHT

Learning the Love Language of the Task-Oriented Person

A task-oriented person is one characterized by the value he/she places on accomplishments, work, possession, or things. In other words, what you do "to" them is not as important as what you do "for" them. To a task-centered husband or wife, actions speak louder than words.

A Time and a Place

Task-oriented people are prone to compartmentalize their lives. For them there is a time and a place for everything as well as for every relationship.

This characteristic can be a great strength to any marriage. Task-centered marriage partners are often more organized and best suited to handling the money. They are inclined to make lists, establish budgets, and live by the appointment book. However, because of their greater expectations, task-oriented people experience great frustration. They are inclined to be perfectionists, or are frustrated because they are not.

There is also a tendency for task-centered people to overcommit themselves in terms of what they can realistically accomplish in a day, a month, or even a lifetime. They are high achievers, and their expectations for their mates and for their children are also great. Herein lies a potential source of conflict and emotional divorce.

The love language of a task-oriented person is largely defined by what he can see accomplished.

For example, Mark came home every day and asked his wife: "What did you do today?" A person who is not task-oriented might have asked a different question such as, "What kind of a day did you have?" But it is often difficult for a task-centered marriage partner to understand the needs of a verbal- or touch-oriented mate inasmuch as task-oriented people often make judgments about their spouse's laziness, unproductiveness and even uselessness.

Mark's wife had spent one day on errands, general clean-up, and in a two-hour phone call with a friend to help the lady with a problem. She felt a sense of accomplishment in helping her friend through an emotional crisis, but Mark exploded in anger when he found out that Sally had spent that long on the phone. To Mark's way of thinking, talking didn't count. As far as he was concerned, his wife had not been productive, and he accused her of being lazy.

Sally responded by calling him an insensitive oaf.

"You don't want me as a person," she exclaimed. "What you want is a cook, a maid, and a prostitute!"

Sally emotionally divorced Mark because she felt unappreciated for what she did, unacceptable to him as a wife, and unloved as a person.

Sally needed to understand Mark as much as Mark needed to understand Sally. It would be easy for a tactile or a verbally-oriented mate to accuse a task-centered partner of being "materialistic," but that would be an injustice and an oversimplification, for we live in a world of symbols, and who is to say that one symbol of security and acceptance is of less or greater value than another?

Mark saw love as a simple matter: You show someone you love her by hard work and effort toward common goals.

As their counselor I talked to Sally about the art of translation: "Mark does love you, Sally. What he is calling into question is your love for him. He wants to see your love translated into action. For example, you can tell Mark that you love him by:

1. Having a clean house.
2. Making sure you remember to buy the ingredients to pack his lunch.
3. Seeing that his clothes are clean and ironed.
4. Having dinner on the table at a certain time every night.
5. Being dependable and on time for appointments.
6. Paying the bills on time.
7. Running errands for him.
8. Working side by side on a project.
9. Doing something special for him such as baking a pie.
10. Mending or repairing a small thing.
11. Being thrifty in the use of money.
12. Giving him a surprise gift with a note expressing appreciation for his hard work."

"It sounds like he wants me to be a slave!" replied Sally.

"There is a difference," I explained, "between service which is motivated by love, and service which is based on intimidation, force, or coercion. Mark would like you to do things because you love him and because you know they please him. Service is seen as an expression of love not servitude.

"Mark is frustrated because he believes that you do not love him and that you do not appreciate his efforts on your behalf. He is willing to work sixteen hours a day in order to provide you with tangible signs of his affection. When he comes home at night and asks you the question, 'What did you do today?' what is he really asking?"

"I don't know," said Sally, "but I feel like I am being put on trial every night. I get to a point where I dread having him walk through the door."

"Would it make any difference," I asked, "if he walked through the door and said, 'Sally, I love you. Do you love me?'"

"Yes," she said. "I think it would. Because of his way of thinking, if I clean house, give birth to his children, cook his meals, etc., I've done something to show my love for him. And he is saying, 'I've worked all day, and in this way I've shown my love for you.'"

"In a very real way that is exactly the intent of Mark's question. Sally, for thirty days I want you to go home and practice being task-responsive. Remember, you may not enjoy the tasks themselves, but perform them as symbols of your love. Meanwhile I'll talk to Mark about appreciating your perspective, about his drill-sergeant attitude."

By the end of the month, significant progress had been made by each of them and they began to be remarried emotionally. The challenge had not disappeared, and yet their willingness sparked an air of excitement and understanding that eventually led them to a new vista of mutual appreciation.

Conditional Love

Task-oriented people tend to offer their love and acceptance conditionally: *If* you do this, *then* I will accept you; *if* you perform this way, *then* I will love you; *if* you do your job, *then* I will appreciate you. Those who conform are favored, and those who do not are rejected, and anyone subjected to constant rejection will either rebel, withdraw, or divorce themselves emotionally.

The dilemma of a task-oriented mate married to a verbal-, touch-, or even to another task-oriented companion is that the task-centered partner says, "I will love you if you perform," and the mate says, "I will perform if I am loved." The solution for the task-centered mate is to be realistic in his expectations, and unconditional in his love.

The non-task-oriented companion needs to be responsive to reasonable requests and appreciative of the efforts of the task-centered mate. Remember, task-centered people frequently prefer the words, "I appreciate you for all you do," rather than the words, "I love you."

If a mate is going to be able to learn the love language of the task-centered person, that mate needs to understand the orientation of the task-centered mate.

The Shortest Distance

Task-oriented people often consider themselves very practical. They stress such undeviating principles as "the shortest distance between two points is a straight line." People, however, are not inanimate points, and the shortest distance may not be a straight line when dealing with human relationships. In other words, the practical is not always the cheapest, the quickest, nor is it a sale item.

Counsel to a Task-Oriented Person

The greatest need of task-oriented people is perspective. The need to prioritize their values. In other words, there needs to be a commitment on the part of the task-oriented person that he will place the husband/wife relationship next only to appropriate individual selfishness. When this relationship becomes just another relationship among many, the task-centered person will lose the emotional support of his companion.

The reason for warning task-oriented persons about perspective lies in the fact that they are, as a group, the most emotionally insensitive. This is not to say that they are devoid of feeling. To the contrary, they feel very strongly. The feelings, however, are not centered in people as much as in things, achievement, accomplishment, work, goals, houses, cars, possessions, money, status, power, etc.

Task-Centered People Need Love, Too

Perspective is a key word because task-centered people also need love, acceptance, and appreciation. Material symbols may provide security for them, but things do not love back. By the time the task-oriented person has achieved his/her objectives in life, the most personal human relationships may have been sacrificed. It need not be that way. Intelligence and management of time, so as to include quality communication with loved ones, will enlist the support of loved ones instead of making enemies of them.

Communicating With the Task-Centered Mate

An important element in communicating with the task-centered mate is agreeing on roles for each mate which define responsibilities. This can be accomplished by sitting down and listing all of the responsibilities necessary for the functioning of the marriage and the family. This is not an easy task, for often there is disagreement on what is necessary and what is nice but nonessential. The key is to share goals, aspirations, and dreams. Dividing up the tasks, according to individual talents and willingness, is the next step. Last, the non-task centered mate must follow through with his assigned tasks.

Making It Happen

To see that emotional fulfillment is not left to cnance, take out the calendar and schedule time for it.

Lynn was a hard-working, self-employed businessman. He seldom put in less than a fourteen-hour day. His wife considered him a "workaholic"—she saw him only late at night, and then he was always tired, short-tempered, and frustrated. His only day off was Sunday, and Lynn would either sleep most of the day, expecting his wife to keep the children quiet, or go off and play golf with his friends.

By the time they came to a family therapist, Lynn's wife had already had an affair with another man. Lynn was deeply hurt, but he wanted to correct whatever was wrong with their marriage.

It was a matter of scheduling. Lynn was so busy trying to put a business together for his family that he lost his wife temporarily.

This couple solved their problem by scheduling time for Lynn to be with the children, and to go on regular weekly dates with his wife. Every other Sunday was family Sunday, and on the alternate Sundays he went golfing or slept. Because both agreed to it, it worked—they made it happen.

The List

Bonnie, a task-oriented mother of four small children, was consistently after her husband John to fix all the little things that aways need fixing around the house. Because John was not a handyman, he didn't even have the inclination to fix things.

To avoid nagging him, Bonnie proposed that a list of the things that needed to be done be kept on a sheet of paper attached to the refrigerator door. Over a period of weeks, the list became longer and longer until a second, third, and finally a fourth sheet were added. Every time John got something out of the refrigerator, he was reminded of the mountainous number of "little things" he needed to do. Finally, he decided to spend two hours every Saturday fixing things, but the list continued to grow and the two-hour period on Saturdays proved inadequate to make even a small dent in the list.

One Saturday, to his wife's surprise, a hired handyman showed up and asked to see the list. John had told him to start at the top of the list and work until he was done. He was not to question the tasks, just do them. John took the children to a football game, and when they returned home in the evening, all the work on the "little things" was done.

At first Bonnie was somewhat upset with John because she felt it wasn't fair. Her expectations were not only that the "little things" be done, but that John do them—that was his role, and to have someone else take over was cheating. However, after talking it over, John and Bonnie decided it wasn't important who did the work as long as it got done.

Then John suggested that a girl be hired to come in once a week and help with heavy cleaning, freeing Bonnie to do other things with her time. Bonnie struggled with feelings of inadequacy, for to bring someone in to help was more or less an admission of her failure. Reason won out, however, and both agreed that in raising a family they would, whenever possible, hire the help they needed.

There are three key points in the foregoing story that are important in communicating with a task-oriented person. First, a list is a great way to communicate expectations (husband to wife, wife to husband, parent to child, or even child to parent), for there they are, in black and white. Second, there are reasonable limits to what any one person can or will do. Third, it is worth a few dollars a week to preserve the energy and time of the task-oriented mate by hiring help for certain chores.

A Gift of Substance

Richard wanted to give Jan a very special gift, something she would remember for a long time. He arranged for a baby tender to come in for a weekend, and made elaborate plans for a weekend in San Francisco, California.

Visions of cable cars, Chinatown, and Fisherman's Wharf danced in his head, but when he announced his intention to Jan, he was disappointed by her reaction. She said she would go if he really wanted her to, but she preferred to take the money and buy a "much needed" rototiller. "A romantic weekend compared to a rototiller?" thought Richard. "It wasn't possible! Nobody would choose a rototiller instead of a trip to San Francisco," and yet, that was precisely what Jan did!

Richard wanted to give Jan a gift that pleased Richard. In many ways it was selfish of him. If you are going to communicate to a task-oriented person, you need to do so in their language.

Wisely, Richard bought the rototiller for Jan, and every time she sees it, she feels appreciative and loving toward her husband.

Hard to Admit

It is often hard for task-oriented persons to admit that they are indeed more task-oriented than tactile or verbal. Part of the reason for this reticence is the value structure of society, for society would have us feel that to be touch- or verbally-oriented is better than being "task" or "thing" oriented. The materialistic heroes of society are seldom loved, even though they may be admired. Consider Howard Hughes, for example.

We seem to have a certain image of the task-oriented person as cold, heartless, uncaring, and without feeling. This, of course, is untrue. The anything-for-love mentality has tended to idealize the touch and verbal nature of a Rhett Butler, while playing down the values of Scarlet O'Hara's commitment to Tara and to the land.

Coming to know and understand our love language, whether it is task, verbal, touch, or a combination of these, is a key to the kind of communication that will eliminate emotional divorce.

Details are Important

Details are an important part of the love language of the task-oriented person.

Fred was romantic, verbal and touch-centered, and Barbara was emphatically task-centered. Through their experience together, Fred knew that Barbara enjoyed dinner at a nice restaurant over almost any other kind of date, and he was in the habit of calling at the last minute and saying, "Let's go out to eat tonight, just the two of us." He enjoyed surprising her.

Barbara, however, did not enjoy being surprised or having to arrange the last minute details. Often she'd harbor feelings of resentment toward Fred. He, of course, felt frustrated.

"I try to do something nice," he said, "and what do I get for it but a slap in the face and a cold shoulder?"

Fred did not understand the art of communicating in the love language of the task-oriented person. An occasional surprise is tolerable, but not preferable to a planned activity where all the details are covered and the "nitty-gritty" taken care of in advance. Generally speaking, task-oriented people enjoy looking forward to an activity. They derive joy in the anticipation as well as in knowing that nothing has been left undone. If Fred had really wanted to impress Barbara, he should have called her on the phone and said, "How does your schedule look for this coming Friday night?"

"It looks fine," Barbara would reply.

"Good," Fred would say, "let's plan on a dinner for two at Captain of the Mar. Hoping you'd be free, I've already phoned and made reservations. Lisa, our baby tender, is free Friday night, and will be happy to tend the baby. You and I should be home by 1:00 a.m."

Heidi, their 14-year-old-daughter wanted to go to the movie Friday night, and Fred thought about that detail, too.

"I've arranged with my mother to drop Heidi and her friend off at the movie and to pick them up afterwards and bring them home. Her friend will not be staying overnight. How does that sound?"

Barbara would be ecstatic at Fred's preparations for the evening. She has not been asked at the last minute and left to arrange not only for a babysitter but everyone else's schedule.

The more order, the greater the peace felt by the task-oriented person. Fred needs to remember that careful planning and preparation are more impressive to a task-centered person than romantic spontaneity.

CHAPTER NINE

Learning the Love Language of the Touch-Oriented Person

Imagine for a moment that you could neither hear nor see nor speak. Touching would instantly become your all-important medium of communication. You would send hundreds of messages which would communicate many different feelings, all through touch.

Decoding the Message

Frequently a non-touch-oriented person will interpret almost any touching gesture as having sexual overtones. This creates a difficult problem in communication. The non-touch-oriented mate needs to understand and accept touching as nonsexual. There are a great number of touch-oriented people who have no ulterior motives in touching other than to communicate friendship, acceptance, and appreciation.

Most people are acquainted with touch-oriented people who are viewed with some suspicion because they are always touching.

Jean, for example, was a touch-oriented woman who was also very talkative and outgoing. When she saw a friend, male or female, she would go over to them, take their arm, and give them a squeeze. In fact, most friends are fortunate if they can escape without also being hugged.

Acceptance was difficult for Jean in her community because several women had been offended by her "friendliness" with their husbands. Although Jean was happily married, these women sincerely felt she was out to get one of their husbands.

In Jean's case, this was not true. On more than one occasion, men reacted by propositioning her, only to find her totally shocked. She has always been faithful to her husband, who accepted her touch-oriented nature as just being herself.

Jean is an attractive woman whose personality is very warm. She is a little naive, and she needs to be more discreet in her touch communication.

There is a place in our society for Jean to be accepted as she has accepted others. Those who understand her frame of reference will come to appreciate her and accept her as a genuine human being.

All hugging and kissing does not have sexual overtones. There are many families where hugging and kissing between brothers and sisters, parents and children, is a common mode of expression. Many touch-oriented people come from these kinds of environments. A touch, hug, or a kiss is intended to be a whole and complete message within itself and not a means to an end.

Counterfeits

There are many counterfeits in society that give a bad name to touch-oriented people. Their sole purpose in life is to seek out a sexual encounter with any one of the opposite sex whom they meet. These people are not well emotionally.

But categorizing all touch-oriented people as "dirty old men or women" is as ridiculous as categorizing all non-touch-oriented people as frigid.

Betty was 34 years old and a divorcee with two children. Her first sexual encounter occurred in the back seat of a car when she was fifteen. She had numerous sexual involvements until her marriage at nineteen, but during her marriage she was a faithful wife. Then, after her divorce, she found herself going from one sexual involvement to another. In fact, she never had a non-sexual relationship with a man. She didn't believe such a relationship could exist. The thought that a man could love her, appreciate her, and be her friend without sex was foreign to her. She thought that all men were alike, interested only in such relationships. Thus she felt that in order for her to be accepted, she had to become sexually involved.

Betty was a dangerous woman, a threat to any relationship. She was incapable of being a friend. When Betty shook hands with a married man, or stood next to a man, her breast touching his arm, her message was calculated and clear. She was not naive. Touching was a means to an end, not an end in itself. Neither Betty nor others like her are truly touch-oriented. They are counterfeits who give a bad name to touch-oriented people.

To Touch or Not to Touch

If a touch-oriented spouse is not free to touch without carrying a sexual message, frustration will invariably follow. It is also frustrating to touch-oriented persons if they are touched only when sexual intercourse is on the mind of their mates.

Tom was twenty-six, married, and the father of one child. A school teacher, he was happily married and true to his wife, who was a homemaker. They both came from traditional backgrounds, and were struggling financially to buy a home.

Whenever Tom was in the same room with his wife, he would touch her, putting his arm around her shoulders or waist, holding her hand or rubbing her back and shoulders. Whenever they were alone in the kitchen, he was inclined to touch her breast or kiss her passionately.

A person married to a touch-oriented mate often feels that the spouse is oversexed, too sexually demanding, and just plain preoccupied with sex. Frequently, the non-touch-oriented partner feels used, resentful, and hostile. The mate's supposed obsession with sex is a source of irritation, and the marital partner finds himself reluctantly condescending to the frequency of sexual encounters, or finding excuses not to become involved.

"I don't feel the need, why should you?" he says and concludes that something is wrong either with him or with his partner.

The Dilemma

A frequent complaint from a non-touch mate is that "it seems that all he wants to do is hug and kiss and go to bed. Sometimes I would like to hug and kiss or just sit together. I resist giving him any encouragement because I know it always leads to bed. There are other things in life I would like to do. I'm not a cold person, but I do resent being touched, grabbed, and handled all the time."

"I enjoy being physically close," replies the touch-centered mate, "and when I make an advance and it is received, I feel it's an all-or-nothing, now-or-never situation. So yes, I admit I encourage an all-the-way attitude."

In a classical conditioning sense, the non-touching mate in the foregoing example has trained his marriage partner to go for broke in order to meet his emotional need for physical closeness; hence, the only time his wife allows herself to be touched is when she agrees to sexual intercourse.

Broaden the Physical Spectrum

The solution to the touch-or-not-to-touch dilemma is to broaden the physical spectrum. The touching mate agrees to let a number of touching experiences such as hugging, kissing, or even fondling, be an end in themselves.

Every physical activity does not have to lead to a more intense activity. If the touching mate will agree to this, then the non-touch-oriented spouse will be more willing to broaden the spectrum of touching. It is also necessary for the non-touching partner to see that sexual intercourse is not a feast or famine situation, but a reasonable part of their shared experience.

It is amazing how compatible and mutually satisfying a marriage can be when the touch-oriented person agrees not to expect all physical touching to lead to sexual intercourse.

When the non-touching partner broadens the physical contact by holding hands, hugging, kissing, fondling, and touching, the need for sexual intercourse actually decreases in the touching mate. The decrease is usually a few weeks in developing. The touching spouse is so conditioned to being turned on by any physical interaction that it takes practice to let hugging and kissing be an end in themselves, but patience and practice will bring compatibility.

"Walk In My Moccasins"

An old Indian proverb declares: "Do not judge another until you have walked in his moccasins." For people who are non-touch-oriented, the following exercise has proven most helpful in creating empathy for their touch-oriented mate.

In order to obtain maximum benefit from this chapter, it is imperative that you at least mentally go through the following experience.

I.   Objective of the Exercise: To communicate by touching alone

II. Materials Necessary: Blindfold, adhesive tape, cotton balls, ear muffs or dish towel, and watch

Rules and Procedure:

1. You cannot speak—this is very important. If you find yourself talking, tape your mouth closed with adhesive tape. It's preferable, however, not to have to tape your mouth.
2. Put cotton balls in your ears, and cover your ears with earmuffs. A dishtowel, worn as a bandana, also works well.
3. Before you are blindfolded, write down each of these words on a separate piece of paper:
    1. Acceptance
    2. Appreciation
    3. Affection
4. Fold the pieces of paper in half so that you cannot read the words, stir them around, pick out one of the pieces of paper and open it so that only you can read it.
5. Your spouse, or another person, sits across from you in a chair with your knees touching.
6. Put on the blindfold.
7. The blindfolded person now has *one minute* to communicate, by touch alone, the feeling listed on the piece of paper.
8. The non-blindfolded person is to write down, on another piece of paper, which one of the three emotions he or she thinks was expressed (appreciation, acceptance, or affection).
9. The blindfolded person quietly returns to his chair, and places his hands on his knees.
10. Repeat the procedure with the other two words.
11. Reverse the roles so that the other person tries the experiment.

You may discover that you do not know how to communicate by touching. It is not even uncommon for one or both of the parties to feel frustration in trying to communicate solely by touching.

This frustration can be productive if it creates empathy for the touch-oriented mate. Many touch-oriented people feel great frustration because their touch messages are either not received or are misinterpreted. As demonstrated by the experiment, it is not always clear what feelings are being expressed. Thus the message sent is not always the message received.

Just as slapping, spanking, or physical abuse communicate rejection, so holding hands, touching, hugging, kissing, petting, and sexual intercourse all communicate acceptance.

In the exercise, "Walk in my Moccasins," how did you communicate *acceptance*? Did you offer to shake hands? Did you reach out and stroke an arm? Did you stand up and give a hug?

If you did any of these, you did well in communicating acceptance, using touch as an end in itself. However, if you used touching as a means of communicating sexual desires, you may need to practice letting *some* touching experiences be ends in themselves. For example, did you run your fingers across his chest in a suggestive way? Did you flirt with his hand with your finger tips? Were there any sexual messages in the touching?

How did you communicate *appreciation* in "Walk in my Moccasins?" Did you reach out and pat your partner's head, shoulder, or hand? Did you squeeze his hand briefly but firmly?

If you did any of the above, you are an effective communicator of appreciation by touch. On the other hand, if any of your touch expressions carried sexual messages, you may need to practice letting touch be an end in itself.

Many people express appreciation through sexual intercourse. It is indeed a kind of reward. This is understandable, but can they also express appreciation through touch that is nonsexual?

A second very important question is this: Did you express appreciation the same way as you expressed acceptance or affection? For example, if you expressed acceptance with hug, and appreciation with a hug also, then the answer is yes, and if your answer is yes, you need to broaden your ability to communicate in the touching realm.

How did you communicate *affection*? Did you stroke his face with your hands? Did you kiss him tenderly? Did you stroke his hands or draw his hands to your chest, neck, or face? If you did any of these, you are an effective communicator of affection using touch as an end in itself.

You will know your intent, that is, whether or not your touch signals were sexual. The issue is whether you can express affection as an end in itself without having that expression carry sexual overtones. This takes practice. It is part of each person's love language to be able to communicate sexually by touch. However, this exercise has focused on a person's acquired skills in the non-verbal world of touching and communicating acceptance, appreciation, and affection as ends in themselves.

Improving the Love Language Skill of the Touch-Oriented Person

Remember that these behaviors are learned, and that it takes practice to increase our awareness and sensitivity. But what a tremendous act of love it is for you to learn to speak your mate's love language. It may be awkward at first, like learning to speak a foreign language. You may make a mistake (you may err a thousand times), but as you gradually improve, you will discover a whole new world of shared experience. You do not need to marry someone completely compatible, but you do need to marry someone who will learn your love language.

This does not mean that a non-touch-oriented person needs to change his personality. He only needs to become aware of and sensitive to his mate's personality. He himself may remain verbal- or task-oriented. But he should develop his ability to understand his companion, to learn a new language, and thereby insure their emotional union.

Touch-Oriented Awareness Exercises

1. Make it a practice to discreetly touch your mate as you pass by, whether in the kitchen, sitting in a chair, or walking down a hallway.

2. When you express verbal appreciation or give a gift, also give a hug, a kiss, or a squeeze of the hand along with the gift.

3. Practice holding your mate tenderly and saying, "I'm not going to say anything. I just want to hold you for a moment."

4. A daily hug and a kiss when you part, and again when you meet, is strong medicine for a touch-oriented mate.

5. Most touch-oriented companions prefer being held to being crushed, not in a bear hug, but in an embrace. Talk about it.

6. Many touch-centered people prefer a kiss of affection to a kiss of passion. Some like both as reasonably often as possible. Ask them.

7. For many touch-oriented mates, sexual intercourse is a process, not an event. They enjoy tender petting and a full measure of foreplay.

8. Holding hands or walking arm-in-arm are great communicators at home or in public.

9. Most touch-centered people sincerely appreciate it when their mate sits next to them in public as well as in private instead of sitting across the room, or being separated in a movie theater by the children. It is not always practical, but it is always appreciated.

10. Back rubs, body massages, and almost any hand-on-body experience is accepted as a token of love. Find out what your spouse thinks.

CHAPTER TEN

Emotional Remarriage and the Sexual Experience

Concern about sexual intimacy is a prime factor in most emotional divorces and a significant consideration for emotional remarriage. Among those currently married, concern about the sexual relationship is a high priority for at least one of the mates. In a majority of marriages, it supersedes concern about money, children, recreation, friends, religion, or in-laws. The sheer physical closeness involved in sexual encounters also intensifies the differences between love languages.

A Great Misunderstanding

It is astounding what great misunderstanding exists between many married couples about the meaning of sexual experience in their marriage.

The cause of this misunderstanding is often founded in the different emotional experiences of the marriage partners as they were growing up in their respective families. For example, if a person who comes from a family that is very touch-oriented, marries a person who comes from a non-touching family, he is often frustrated about marital sex-life.

The question arises: "What does sexual intercourse really represent?"

Is Sex a Physical Need?

Though it is by no means universal, it is very common for a woman, raised in the setting of a traditional home, to view the sexual relationship as a duty which she must fulfill in order to meet her husband's physical needs. Typically, such a woman is shocked to discover that the sexual experience for her husband is more of an emotional need than an experience in physical gratification.

Generally, the husband or wife who is touch-oriented enjoys the full range of physical expression, including touching, holding hands, hugging, kissing, petting, and sexual intercourse.

Task-oriented people tend to compartmentalize their sex life—there is a time and a place for everything. It is often annoying or embarrassing to them to deal with sexual matters or feelings outside of the bedroom.

Most verbally-centered people enjoy a full measure of conversation, and the sexual experience is enhanced by talking about it before, during, and after the experience.

One husband said this about his basic frustration over the sex life in his marriage:

"She is always available, but somehow I feel she is not really there. Oh, I don't believe she is thinking of anyone else, but she is so passive that I feel very little satisfaction and a great deal of frustration."

Later, when I visited with the wife alone and inquired about her observations concerning her husband's sexual fulfillment, she made this comment: "Well, he has nothing to complain about in that department because I am always available to him."

I asked her if she thought the relationship was emotionally fulfilling to her husband.

"What do you mean?" she asked.

"Let's invite your husband back into this conversation," I said.
He came in and sat down.

"Tell your wife," I said, "what you related to me about her being available for sexual intercourse.

"I told him," said the husband, "that it wasn't enough to know that you were available. Somehow, I feel you are too passive and I am frustrated after intercourse."

"Well," she said, very defensively, "I can't be anybody but who I am. I'm not a prostitute, and I don't believe in those sex manuals. You ought to be grateful I'm always available. I just don't understand you."

At that point, I made an observation: "What your husband is talking about is not physical intercourse, but emotional intercourse. Ironically, physical intercourse without emotional commitment is prostitution. Your husband does not want a prostitute. He is looking for emotional fulfillment through a physical medium.

"Many women like yourself have been taught that a good wife is one who cares for the sexual needs of her husband by being available. But availability is only a part of the sexual experience. To have sexual intercourse without some emotional interaction is a form of rejection. For most people it is incredibly degrading and frustrating. I am not going to suggest any sex manuals for you, but I am going to suggest that you need to change your attitude about your sexual relationship with your husband. Attempt to have emotional intercourse, not just physical intercourse. This means more than being physically active; it means being emotionally active."

We reviewed the "art of receiving" and her need to focus on the message, give 100% attention to the messenger, express appreciation, and be sincere.

Many men and women substitute the frequency of intercourse for emotional intercourse, only to find that they are still unfulfilled. Seldom are sexual needs equal in a marriage, and therefore, one partner is called upon to be more giving. Frequently the giving partner will soon begin to feel used, and begin to resent his mate. Subconsciously, the mate feeling used will begin to punish the other with passive sex, and the relationship is doomed to mutual frustration unless there can be an attitude adjustment.

Sex as Acceptance

Suppose, as with the woman above, we were to place her in a chair and say, "You cannot leave the chair until you feel overwhelmed with the need for physical gratification through sexual means." I suggested this during the interview and the husband responded, "Hell would freeze over and the devil would learn to ice skate first."

It is important to realize that not everyone sees the sexual experience as necessary in meeting emotional needs. Nunneries and monastaries are a testimony to that fact. It is also true that sex is not a basic physical need, or else people would be dying every year for lack of sexual intercourse. (The woman in the foregoing example commented that her husband would be the first to die.) Even so, divorce files involving sexual infidelity, in quest of emotional acceptance, are myriad.

Sexual intercourse often becomes the barometer to measure the density of emotional acceptance. Many marriage partners can have a knock-down, drag-out verbal brawl and then, to the great dismay of their spouse, expect to go to bed and have sexual intercourse. Why? Willingness to have sexual intercourse represents for many people the basic emotional need for acceptance. If someone is married to a person who views sexual intercourse as acceptance, it becomes important to the relationship to learn that partner's love language.

The Sexual Experience and the Task-Oriented Mate

Learning the love language of the task-centered person is a

matter of understanding his frame of reference. Once you have decoded his language, you are in a position to send a thousand messages of love, but until you learn his love language, you are speaking in a foreign tongue.

Task-centered people tend to compartmentalize their sex life. There is a time and a place for everything, and sex is no different.

Diane, for example, was very blunt in her reaction to her sex life with her husband.

"I am like a service station," she said. "I feel very little, if any, emotional involvement. When we were first married, I felt different. I was in love with him, and I felt that sexual intercourse was a mutual expression of love. Now I just don't know. I feel used. He has the attitude that I should be ready, twenty-four hours a day, to jump into bed wih him. I feel like a call girl. He doesn't seem to care about the children's music lessons, dinner, or anything except sex. I resent him because I think he is selfish. What about my schedule? What about the things that I have planned and organized? If they aren't important, then I'm not important. I feel a sense of responsibility to other people and to other things. He is irresponsible and couldn't care less for anything except sex.

"The other day he came home unexpectedly for lunch and wanted to go to bed with me. I was supposed to be flattered; instead, I was frustrated. He has no consideration whatsoever for anyone but himself. It also bothers me that if I don't give in to his sexual desires, he pouts and sulks around just like a child. Later, I get the silent treatment or no cooperation. I can't put up with that kind of intimidation and immaturity. Our marriage is a one-way street and I think it's a dead end."

Diane was a task-centered person. Her husband was obviously not speaking her love language. He had succeeded in doing the very opposite of what he had intended. Instead of communicating, "I love you, I care about you, and I want to be with you," he communicated, "I don't love you, I care only about myself, and I couldn't care less what your schedule is."

The more passive his wife became, the more insistent and demanding he became. Eventually, they sought a divorce.

As a family court commissioner, I was assigned their case by the judge, and after counseling with them, I was able to help them agree to a three-month probationary time. During the three months, they were to seriously attempt to communicate in the love language of their mate.

The husband agreed to the following counsel: "When communicating with a task-oriented mate, remember that only rarely will romantic spontaneity be as impressive as a planned event. Schedule it to happen at a time and a place when and where it is convenient for her. Task-centered individuals find more joy in anticipation than in surprise. Because of the compartmentalized nature of most task-oriented people, you will also find that your mate will be mentally prepared to focus on your sexual encounter. Otherwise, you may find that you have her body, but not her emotions or her mind. Without proper notice, she will be preoccupied with thoughts of what needs to be done that isn't being done because she is in bed.

Instead of enjoying the sexual experience, she will be more frustrated than ever because of the unmet expectations she had for the time now taken away by sexual intercourse.

I told her husband, "In your love language, spur-of-the-moment sexual encounters are flattering, but to her they are more of an insult because they demonstrate, to her way of thinking, a lack of consideration for her schedule. Task-centered people are turned on by planning, lists, schedules, organization, and attention to detail.

"What you are currently doing is not meeting your needs or hers. Your wife is not rejecting sexual intercourse, she is rejecting your approach, and unless you can change your approach, she will also reject you.

"Assume for a moment that a man would like to be with his task-oriented wife, sexually, during his lunch break. Learning to communicate in her love language would require him to plan *with* her in order for such an encounter to happen so that she will be mentally and emotionally prepared."

After inquiring which day in the week she is free, the husband confirms, "You've got yourself a date! I'll phone and make reservations for 11:00 at the restaurant. I'll pick you up at 10:45 sharp. We should be home by 12:00, and ready for 'something else.' I love you, Diane."

"I'll be ready. I love you, too, and I really appreciate your consideration for my schedule."

There are many people who would think that the counsel was a bit much. Surely being that specific isn't necessary. And yet it is usually appreciated by the task-centered individual.

There is wisdom, pure and simple, in planting the idea of the encounter in the mind of the task-centered individual if you wish to reap the harvest. Not all sexual encounters need to be explicitly mapped out, but they should be mutually agreed upon. Often a word in the morning, or a phone call during the day is sufficient. The task-oriented person needs to be able to plan.

"Tonight after the children are asleep, let's get together," or "I just called to see if you would be interested in one fantastic night of love?"

Why is planning or scheduling a sexual experience so important to a task-centered mate? The answer is pacing. Long distance runners are trained to pace themselves in order to complete a race. A runner's finest effort results from a fast pace which reserves sufficient energy for a burst of speed at the end. A characteristic of many task-oriented people is their pacing.

A danger, previously noted, for many task-centered people is their tendency to overschedule and overplan. They are often unrealistic about what can be accomplished in twenty-four hours. There are a certain number of tasks which need to be performed during the day, and there is only so much time and energy available for accomplishing the task. Frequently, the task-centered mate will measure out energy to meet the task and then collapse in bed exhausted. The mate may have been thinking all day about a sexual encounter at night, only to be frustrated by the words, "I'm just too tired tonight."

By planting the idea in the mind of the task-centered person, she will be able to pace her day accordingly. She may decide to take a nap, or to pace her workload so there will be sufficient energy to finish the day and still have sufficient physical and emotional energy to enjoy sexual intercourse.

The Sexual Experience and the Touch-Oriented Mate

For most touch-centered individuals, sexual intercourse is only a part of a very complete world of touching. It is often difficult for a non-touch person to extend themselves enough to be able to speak in the love language of their touch-centered mate. They feel awkward, embarrassed, or uncertain. Touching is a foreign language for many. In a similar manner, those who study foreign languages are often reluctant to speak that language when they actually visit the country. They fear they will mispronounce a word or be misunderstood. Some are afraid others will make fun of them.

Non-touching people often feel these same concerns. They possess the words, but they lack the confidence to use them. The lack of confidence experienced by a non-touching person is often reinforced when they assert themselves to over-reaction, only to find their efforts unacceptable. Grabbing and bear hugging, though definitely "touching" experiences, are seldom appreciated. Yelling and screaming are also verbal forms of communication, yet they do not meet the needs of the verbal-centered person.

Non-touching mates frequently use a limited touching vocabulary. When non-touch people think of touching, they think only of the hands. The range of touching includes the whole body—the tongue, the nose, the lips, the arms, the legs, the feet, etc. Just being held is incredibly important to most touch-centered mates.

Touching can be a highly sophisticated, non-verbal language. Distinct messages can be sent—touches of affection, touches of friendship, and touches of appreciation. Few interpret a handshake as anything but a gesture of friendship. Hugging, however, carries different messages, depending on the messenger. There are hugs of acceptance and hugs of affection, and there are those who do not know the difference.

Jim was a touch-centered husband. His wife was task-oriented, and it was difficult for her to understand his need for touching. She often pulled away from him in embraces, and she was always the one to conclude a kiss. They shared sexual intercourse two or three times a week, and she was baffled by his feeling that she would never be able to meet his needs.

Jim wondered if something were wrong with him. Why did he feel the need to touch? A quick glance into his background was sufficient. Jim came from a home where both his mother and father were touch-oriented. Hugs and kisses were the order of the day. He was hugged and kissed when he left for school and when his dad left for work. Jim's parents were always holding hands, sitting together, walking arm in arm, or touching in one way or another. When the children returned home in the afternoon, they were greeted with a hug and a kiss, and a few hours later when dad returned home, everybody greeted him likewise. Whenever Jim was hurt, or whenever he returned home with a good report card, he was hugged and kissed.

Touching was a part of Jim. It was an important medium of communication in his family as he was growing up, and so it was important for him in marriage. He was a very loving father, and yet he felt rejected by his wife.

The first thing I said to Jim's wife was this: "Let Jim embrace you and hold you, and let him be the one to determine when the embrace is over."

She expressed concern that he would hold on forever, but I assured her that there was a difference between a quality hug and a quick grab in the mind of a touch-oriented person.

From her point of view, a hug was an event, and once you had embraced, all the messages were sent and it was time to get on with other things.

For Jim a hug was a deeply satisfying emotional experience, and there were different hugs for different messages. Jim's feelings of rejection were directly associated with the fact that his wife had actually pushed him away during a hug.

I counseled her to learn to relax during an embrace, and to concentrate on a quality hug.

"Don't be in a hurry to get it over and move on to other things. When Jim embraces you from behind in the kitchen, take your hands and place them on his hands. Pat his hands as a sign of acceptance. When you have your arms around each other, rub his back or gently press yourself against him until he terminates the embrace. The extra minute it will take to say hello or goodbye will pay dividends in assurance far in excess of the time involved.

"Second, the same principle of withdrawing holds true for kissing. Let Jim terminate the kiss. Your withdrawal is a form of rejection."

Jim was counseled to be reasonable in the duration of his kisses. The couple was to return in three months and report their progress.

The time passed quickly and when they came into the office the result was self-evident. They wore expressions of love, and I knew that they had emotionally remarried. Jim was fulfilled, happy, content, and attentive to his wife, and in return she was radiant.

It was interesting to note that the frequency of sexual intercourse did not increase or decrease. It had never been a matter of the frequency of touching or the frequency of sexual intercourse. It had been a matter of the quality of the touching experience.

The Sexual Experience and the Verbally-Oriented Person

For the verbally-centered person, the sexual experience is enhanced by talking about it before, during, and after the encounter. This does not mean that sex is the only thing that is talked about, for it is not sex, but the individual that is the focus.

Verbally-oriented people want to make love verbally as well as physically. The difference between a sexual relationship without conversation and one with verbal communication is the difference between eating and dining.

Bob, for example, was a verbally-centered husband, Lucy was a quiet, task- and touch-oriented wife.

Bob was always asking Lucy to tell him about how she felt about their sex life.

"Fine," was all Lucy would say. It was embarrassing for her to talk about it. She felt awkward using words with sexual meanings. Even when just the two of them were alone, she had difficulty expressing her feelings verbally.

Bob was frustrated. He wanted Lucy to tell him what she enjoyed and what she did not enjoy sexually. He wanted feedback during intercourse and approval afterward. As a result, Lucy was sexually satisfied and fulfilled, while Bob was extremely frustrated, and considered their sex life a disaster.

In counseling with Lucy, I tried to point out that Bob's frustration was concentrated in two areas. First, Bob wanted Lucy to receive all of his love. He had a two-part gift, and Lucy was receiving only half of his gift. Though she was satisfied with their sex life, he wasn't, because she turned him off by not allowing him to make love to her verbally. She needed to practice the art of receiving by encouraging him whenever he talked to her about the love life. Secondly, Bob felt a deep need to be verbally reinforced. He needed to be told that he was appreciated. He wanted to hear that the sexual experience was pleasurable and satisfying.

Bob was already feeling emotionally divorced, and it was my prediction that he would have a mistress in a matter of months if things did not change at home.

Lucy decided that her verbal insecurities were not worth as much as the marriage, and she agreed to follow counsel.

Before

To eat or to dine, that is the question, Dining is a quality experience which often includes hor d'oeuvres. An example of a verbal hors d'oeuvre would be for Lucy to call Bob on the phone and say, "I love you madly. I can hardly wait for you to come home and make love to me."

I counseled Bob to be willing to let Lucy experiment and to be patient with her. Her willingness to try was really appreciated by Bob, and he agreed to continue to be verbally active and not just wait for Lucy to perform.

I explained to Lucy that Bob wanted to be verbally flirtatious. She needed to encourage his sexual conversation. This did not mean, however, that she needed to be vulgar or crude. On the contrary, the two of them could take great pleasure in being discreet in developing a love language all their own, complete with the clue words, pet names, and dual meanings.

Being able to enjoy verbal foreplay hours before sexual inter-course would meet Bob's need for assurance that their sex life was mutual. He needed to know that Lucy was a willing partner, and that he was not imposing his will on her in a one-sided affair.

During

It is often difficult for a non-verbal person to talk about sexual feelings during intercourse. Many non-verbal people will talk during intercourse, but not about sexual feelings. They will talk about problems, children, business, the weather, but not the sexual act. Incredible as it sounds, this happens consistently in many marriages. Talking about other things during intercourse is a form of rejection, and tells a mate that intercourse is not on their mind; that it is secondary to whatever they are talking about.

It is important to realize that most verbally-centered people want to know how they are performing sexually.

After

I explained that Bob would want to talk about the sexual experience afterwards, while Lucy might be inclined to silence.

The verbally-active person derives satisfaction and emotional reinforcement from discussion. The sexual act itself is often not as important as the emotional environment which surrounds it. Being able to talk about it made Bob secure and confident.

As a counselor, I recommended to Lucy that she mention to Bob either the same night or the next day in a phone call that "everything last night was wonderful. I just wanted you to know." If Lucy were more outgoing, she might respond with "You are a fantastic lover. Let's get together again soon."

The story of Bob and Lucy has a happy ending because of their mutual willingness to communicate in their mate's love language. Every married person needs to study his mate's love language. By knowing the language couples are better able to communicate and possibilities for emotional divorce are lessened.

Relationships are Different

Relationships are different. Our affinity to be touch-, task- or verbally-oriented may vary from one relationship to another. A husband may be touch-verbal with his wife, verbal-task with some of his children and task-verbal with his parents. The nature of the relationship we develop with another may actually define our use of touch, task or verbal. Although it is generally true we develop a basic disposition of being touch-, task-, or verbal-centered, which tends to spill over into all of our primary relationships, it is wise to look at the nature of each relationship and treat it as an independent identity.

Perspective

This book has concerned itself with the husband-wife relationship. Our focus has been in understanding and defining our mates' love language as well as our own.

The terms "touch," "task" and "verbal" are labels which can be misused and lead to an oversimplification of our complex natures. Therefore, it is important to remember they are not a panacea to solve all communication problems between loved ones. Rather, they are useful tools which may assist us in defining how to effectively communicate in a manner which avoids emotional divorce.

When both partners in a marriage are willing to communicate in their mate's love language, not only is emotional divorce avoided but also emotional bonding is maintained. An emotional bonding is an absolute necessity in a healthy marriage relationship.